Starring Alice MacKenzie

Narinder Dhami

Collins
An imprint of Harper Collins*Publishers*

First published in Great Britain by
Collins 1996
1 3 5 7 9 10 8 6 4 2

Collins is an imprint of
CollinsChildren'sBooks, part of
HarperCollins*Publishers* Ltd,
77-85 Fulham Palace Road,
Hammersmith, London W6 8JB

ISBN 0 00 675135-0

Printed and bound in Great Britain by
HarperCollins Manufacturing, Glasgow

STARRING ALICE MACKENZIE

'Morning, love.' The postman was holding out a couple of letters from the doorstep. 'Here's your post.'

I looked at him, bewildered.

'Why didn't you push it through the letterbox like you usually do?'

'Oh, it's the personal touch.' The postman was doing strange things with his head. He was craning his neck from one side to the other as if he was in pain or something. 'Got to keep my customers happy.'

'Have you a bad neck?' I asked him politely.

'What? Oh, no.' Now he was squinting over my shoulder towards the kitchen. 'That TV crew arrived yet?'

Then it clicked. I should have realised from the look on his face. Another victim of Telly Fever.

Well, there was no way I was going to get it, anyway. Or was there?

Also available from Collins

Paper Faces *Rachel Anderson*
The Indian in the Cupboard *Lynne Reid Banks*
A Dangerous Place *Janice Brown*
Angel Face *Narinder Dhami*
Bottle Boy *Stephen Elboz*
Street Child *Berlie Doherty*
The Girls' Gang *Rose Impey*
The Other Way Round *Judith Kerr*
A Devil to Ride *Patricia Leitch*
Little House on Rocky Ridge *Roger Lea MacBride*
Sweet 'n' Sour *Nina Milton*
The Silver Crown *Robert O'Brien*
Apple Bough *Noel Streatfeild*

Chapter One

The radio was on full blast, but nobody could hear it. This is not unusual in our house on a Monday morning at breakfast-time. If a Trident missile had dropped through our roof and landed nose-down in the cornflakes box, no one would have noticed.

'Doh, re, mi, fah, soh, la, te, DOH!!!' That's my mum, burning the toast and practising her scales. No, she isn't an opera singer. She's a member of the Wolverhampton Amateur Lyrical Larks Society. Or WALLIES for short. They do all sorts of shows and nothing ever fazes Mum. She was a nun in *The Sound of Music* once, and even when she tripped over her habit, and fell into the orchestra pit she just climbed out (with a hand from the piano player) and carried on singing. The audience went wild. I've got to say it: even though she's my mum, she's a bit of a show-off.

'One-nil! How could they lose one-nil to that bunch of flat-footed oiks!' That's my dad, reading the paper and having his morning moan, as well as a sneaky cigarette (he's supposed to have given up). Dad's football mad. He supports the Wolves, and if they lose, it depresses him so much that he has to have a lie-down on the sofa with a couple of cans of beer. At least that's what *he* says. Dad's a bus driver now, but when he was a kid he really wanted to be a footballer. He did have a trial for the Wolves when he was sixteen, but he just didn't make it. Even now, after all these years, I think he still gets a bit choked when he remembers that. According to Dad, though, if Wolves *had* seen sense and taken him on, they'd have won the World Cup, The Ashes and the Oxford v Cambridge Boat Race by now.

'Oh, MUM! Isn't it possible to get a piece of toast in this house that hasn't been cremated?'

Meet Cindy, my fifteen-year-old sister. She's blonde and slim and pretty and she's got a mouth on her the size of the Channel Tunnel. She's the teen drama queen of the West Midlands (and probably of the world as well). Nobody, but nobody, can ever get the better of Cindy in an argument. That's why we all keep quiet when she does her nails at the kitchen table, like she's doing now. It's pretty disgusting, but it's not as bad as the time she was putting on her make-up when we were having dinner, and she dropped a false eyelash into the lasagne. Dad thought it was a spider and hit it with his spoon, and we all ended up covered in tomato sauce.

'Dead fingers touch my face . . .' That's my brother Jools muttering strangely under his breath, and writing yet another song on the back of the cornflakes box. He's fourteen, and he wants to be a rock star, so he's always in his bedroom, fiddling with his electric guitar. Unfortunately, he can't actually *play* the electric guitar, but Jools says that's just a technicality. When he was born, my dad wanted to name him after the Wolves side who won the League Cup in 1980, but Mum put her foot down. However, my brother thinks Julian is the worst name in the history of the planet, so we have to call him Jools, or he practically foams at the mouth. Cindy calls him Julian whenever she wants to wind him up. Which is often.

'What rhymes with "face"?' Jools looked at us over the top of his shades. He always wears dark glasses and black clothes, and he painted his bedroom black last week. Dad says it's like living with Dracula.

'Headcase,' Cindy said helpfully.

'Funny.' Jools reached across the table to flick her on the nose, and knocked the milk bottle over. 'Oh, b—.'

'Mind your language,' Mum cut in automatically.

'Blast!' Jools started trying to mop the puddle of milk up with the sleeve of his school sweater.

'If you took those sunglasses off once in a while, you might be able to see what you were doing, my lad,' Dad muttered from behind his newspaper.

'Dad, you just don't know the meaning of cool!' Jools snapped. 'Yeeaagh!'

Our cats, Buster and Bully, had dived for the stream of milk dripping onto the floor, and were fighting it out under the table, biting whatever got in their way. In this case, Jools' ankles.

So now you've met everybody. Except me. I'm just Alice. I'm eleven years old, I've got straight, mousy-brown hair and I'm pretty ordinary.

Anyway, like I said before, this morning was just like any other morning in the Mackenzie household. Loud. I was sitting in my usual place on the stool near the window, writing in my notebook. Or Alice Jane Mackenzie's Private and Top Secret Notebook, to be precise. I write down all sorts of things in my notebook – stories, poems, things that have happened to me (not that anything much ever does). Today I was writing a story about a girl whose pet dog dies, but he comes back as a ghost, and helps her catch a burglar.

Well, it sounded like a good idea when I first thought of it . . .

I was sitting near the radio, but I wasn't really listening to it. I've learnt how to block loud noises out of my head when I'm writing. You have to when you live in this house. But all of a sudden something about the way the DJ was talking caught my attention.

'Right, I've got an important message for any of you folk listening out there who fancy being TV STARS!' I raised my eyebrows, and looked at the radio. DJs usually get all over-excited about nothing in particular, but this actually sounded quite interesting, for once. 'Harlequin TV are looking for a typical, normal British family to appear in a new 'fly-on-the-wall' documentary series about family life in the 1990s. You must be willing to let the TV cameras into your home, and be prepared to let your everyday life be filmed, warts and all. Interested? If you are, I've got a phone number here for you to call, so grab a pen and paper . . .'

I sucked my pen thoughtfully. That sounded interesting. Maybe I should write the number down, just in case . . . Then I hesitated. No, maybe not. I quite fancied the idea of being on TV, but I wasn't sure about being filmed at home, 'warts and all'. That sounded a bit dodgy to me.

Suddenly I became aware that the kitchen had gone quiet. This was so unusual that I looked up from my notebook. Dad was scribbling the phone number down on his newspaper, Jools was doing the same on the cornflakes box, Mum was writing it feverishly on the wipe-clean memo board, and Cindy was painting it in red nail varnish on the back of her hand. The silence lasted for about three seconds (about the maximum in this house), and then everyone burst out talking at once.

'Dad!' Cindy squealed. 'Dad, we can ring up, can't we?'

'Excellent!' said Jools. 'D'you think we'd be in with a chance?'

'What do you think, Dan?' My mum looked eagerly at my dad.

'Hold on a minute,' I said quickly. But nobody heard me. They don't usually. Not at first, anyway.

'Me – on the telly!' Cindy was already tossing her hair back, and making eyes at an imaginary camera. 'It'll be ace!'

'Okay, calm down, we haven't been chosen yet,'

said my dad, his eyes shining with hope. 'It'd be great if we were though, eh, Babs?'

'Absolutely brilliant!' said my mum. 'That'd show that old bag Marjorie Carter down at WALLIES. She thinks she's the dog's dinner ever since she beat me for the lead role in *Oklahoma*!'

I got up and turned the radio off.

'Quiet!' I said firmly.

Silence. Four pairs of eyes swivelled round to look at me.

'What's up, squirt?' Cindy asked, looking surprised.

'You mean you lot *really* want to go in for this TV thing?' I asked, looking round at them. They all stared back at me. What a stupid question. Of course they did.

'You mean you *don't* want to?' said Cindy and Jools together, looking stunned.

'I didn't say that.' I hesitated for a moment, trying to work out exactly what my feelings were. Of course I wanted to be on TV – didn't everybody? I'd daydreamed about being on TV loads and loads of times, imagining that I was grown-up and a famous writer, and everyone wanted me to appear on their chat show, and talk about my latest book. But the idea of a film crew in *our* house, watching and filming our every private move, didn't sound so great to me.

Dad was looking hard at me. He had a great thing about doing everything 'as a family'.

'So how d'you feel about it, Ally? We can't go ahead unless we're all in this together.'

'Alice, you're not going to say no, are you?' groaned Cindy. 'This is our big chance to be TV stars!'

My whole family stared hopefully at me. You know how in cartoons, dollar signs pop in people's eyes when they see a big heap of money? Well, right now I could see star signs clicking up in everybody's eyes. Click. Click. Click. Click. They all wanted to *be* somebody, and this was their big chance. Or at least they thought it was. I shook my head, almost laughing out loud.

'Do you realise how many families are going to go in for this thing?' I asked, raising my eyebrows. 'We haven't got a hope of being chosen —'

I was immediately shouted down.

'Of course we have!' Cindy argued enthusiastically. 'We're interesting, talented and gorgeous! Even Jools is okay, if you're into pale, skinny guys who look like death warmed up —'

'Thanks a lot,' Jools growled. 'Anyway, we've got just as good a chance as anyone else.'

'It can't hurt to give it a go,' Mum said determinedly.

I shrugged. I know when I'm beaten. When the Mackenzies have got a scheme in hand, it's best just to let them get on with it (and be around to pick up the pieces later on).

'OK, then. I don't mind,' I said with a grin. And I didn't really, because a) secretly I quite fancied the idea of being on the telly, and b) it was blindingly obvious to just about anyone with half a brain that we weren't going to get chosen anyway.

Everyone cheered. Cindy rushed round the table, and gave me a big hug, Jools slapped me on the back and Mum went off to make some more burnt toast to celebrate. Only Dad stayed still, looking at me.

'Ally, are you *really* sure about this, love?' he asked quietly.

Dad knows me better than anyone, and I think he could see that maybe I wasn't *quite* so enthusiastic as everyone else. That was because there was one big difference between me and the rest of my family. They all firmly believed that they were born to be stars, and me, I didn't think I even came close. Don't get me wrong. I wanted desperately to be a star too, but secretly, deep down, I didn't really believe I stood a chance. When I was six years old we went on holiday to Butlins, and Mum entered us all in a family talent contest. We were supposed to sing 'The Birdie Song', and do all the actions, but I burst into tears when I saw everyone in the audience looking at me, and I had to be taken off the stage by a Redcoat. The rest of the family carried on without me, and won first prize. That just about sums up the difference between me and them.

'I'm fine, Dad. Honestly. But there *is* one thing —' I glanced round at my starstruck family '— I don't think we should tell anyone we're going in for this TV programme.'

Cindy and Jools both stopped in mid-charge to the phone in the hall, and Mum looked round from the toaster.

'Why not?' Cindy and Jools demanded, both looking distinctly put out.

'I just don't think it's a good idea,' I said firmly. Damage limitation was what I was aiming for here. The way I saw it, we weren't going to be chosen anyway, so there didn't seem much point in going around telling everybody we were going to be on the telly, and then feeling like right prats when we had to tell them we *weren't*. I didn't think Cindy and Jools were going to agree at first, but then a calculating gleam came into Cindy's eyes.

'She's right, you know, Jools,' she said slowly. 'If we tell too many people at school, maybe they'll go in for it too, and then we've got less chance of being chosen . . .'

Jools nodded. 'Yeah, that's true.'

I breathed a silent sigh of relief. The fewer people who knew about this, the better. In a couple of weeks' time another family would have been chosen, everybody would be disappointed and we could all go back to normal. Normal for Mackenzies, anyway.

I stood up as there was a knock at the back door.

'That'll be Francine.' I jumped off the stool, and gave everyone a warning look. 'Don't tell her about the TV.'

They all nodded virtuously.

I opened the back door, and my best mate Francine sloped into our kitchen, yawning.

'Ready for school, Mackenzie?' she said.

At least, that's what I think she said. It was difficult to hear over Cindy's deafening screech.

'Francine! Guess what? We're going to be on the telly!'

'We *might* be on the telly,' Jools interrupted.

'Oh, nothing's settled yet,' said Mum. 'But I think we're in with a good chance.'

And then everyone was talking at once.

I shook my head in despair, then I caught Dad's eye, and I couldn't help giggling. Trying to gag Cindy was like trying to keep a herd of mad elephants quiet.

Francine's eyes were standing out on stalks.

'Wow! You lucky things!' she gasped. 'Hey, Alice, d'you think my family could apply? I'd love to be on the telly!'

'See?' I said triumphantly to Cindy. 'If you go round blabbing about it to everybody, they'll all want to go in for it.'

'Oh, well, Francine doesn't count,' said Cindy airily. 'She's almost like one of the family anyway.'

'Er – thanks,' said Francine doubtfully, obviously not quite sure whether this was a compliment or not.

I giggled.

'I'll just get my bag, France.'

I went out of the kitchen and into the hall, still laughing. My family are incredible. Sometimes I feel like I'm the sensible parent, and they're all the naughty kids.

'Ally?' Dad came out of the kitchen behind me. 'Sure you're all right, love?'

I looked at him. I can always tell when Dad's worried about me by this funny little frown he gets, right between his eyebrows, and he was frowning now.

'Honestly, Dad, I'm fine,' I said patiently, pulling my bag out of the hall cupboard.

Dad didn't look totally convinced.

'Come, on, Ally, you can tell me. If you hate the whole idea of this TV thing, I'll stop it right now.'

''Course I don't hate it! I'd love to be on the telly...' I thought for a second or two, wanting to be honest with Dad about how I really felt. 'OK, I think the idea of the TV people coming to film in our house is a bit off. I'd like it better if we were going to be interviewed at the TV studios or something. But . . .' I shrugged. 'It's not going to happen anyway, is it? We're not going to get chosen out of all those hundreds and hundreds of other families who're going to apply, whatever Cindy thinks.'

'No, I suppose you're right.' Dad looked a bit depressed, like a small child who's had his favourite toy removed. 'I think we all got a bit carried away . . .'

'A bit?' I repeated, smiling at him. Dad smiled back.

'OK, a lot!' he admitted. 'Well, as long as you're not worrying about it . . .'

'I'm not.' I kissed his cheek, and we went back into the kitchen. 'Come on, Francine. 'Bye, everybody.'

No one heard me. Mum had started going on at Dad to have the house decorated, ready for the filming, and Cindy and Jools were already arguing about which one of them was going to be more popular with the viewing millions. I shook my head sadly as Francine and I went out of the back door. In true Mackenzie style, this whole thing was getting rapidly out of hand already, and we hadn't even applied yet. I just hoped they weren't going to be incredibly disappointed when we weren't chosen.

'Alice Jane Mackenzie, why aren't you jumping up and down and screaming at the top of your voice?' Francine demanded as we went down the alley between the gardens. 'If I was going to be on the telly, I'd be turning cartwheels down the street! Aren't you excited?'

''Course I am.' It was true. The idea of seeing myself on a TV screen made me go all shivery with excitement inside. But, as I'd tried to explain to Dad, it wasn't as simple as that. 'I'm just not sure if I want to be filmed at home.'

'Why not?' Francine was looking at me curiously.

I shrugged helplessly. I wanted to explain to Francine exactly how I felt, but it sounded pretty wet. To me, home was a private place, somewhere familiar but somewhere special too. The thought of strangers being able to switch on their TV set, and watch me living my normal, everyday life at home made me feel a bit funny inside. How could you feel the same about home, if millions and millions of people were watching you sitting in your living room, eating egg and chips?

'Well, it's not very private, is it?'

'You mean they might want to film you *in the bathroom* or something?' Francine shuddered. 'Yuk! Gross!'

That hadn't been exactly what I meant, but I couldn't find the words to explain how I was really feeling inside.

'Anyway,' I went on. 'Do you know how many families are going to apply for this thing? Hundreds, maybe thousands, that's how many. We haven't got a hope of being chosen –'

Francine wasn't listening. She was staring down at my shoulder, her eyes huge with terror.

'Alice!' she croaked. 'Don't move! There's a ginormous spider on your arm!'

I squinted down.

'No, it isn't,' I said, picking it neatly off my school jumper. 'It's another one of Cindy's escaped eyelashes. It must've come off when she hugged me.'

Francine and I looked at each other, and burst out laughing.

'I think my family must be the weirdest bunch in the whole world,' I said, shaking my head. 'You know what that man on the radio said this morning?'

'No, what?'

'He said the TV company were looking for a typical, normal British family.' I grinned at Francine. 'Well, my family aren't typical. And they're definitely not normal.'

Francine's face fell.

'You mean you don't think you'll be chosen?'

'I bet you a million pounds we won't be,' I said confidently.

Chapter Two

'Maybe there'll be a letter or something from the TV company today, when you get home,' Francine said hopefully, as we walked out of the school playground. 'Or maybe they'll have rung your mum . . .'

As Francine had said this almost every single day for the past few weeks, ever since we'd applied to be on the TV programme, I didn't bother answering her. I had other things on my mind.

Today had been a bad day. For a start, our class teacher, Miss Munro, had had another row with her boyfriend. We always knew when Miss Munro had had a row with her boyfriend the night before, because she stormed round the classroom like an Exocet missile, mowing down anyone and everything in her path. I'd forgotten my PE kit, so I was lucky to get out of the classroom alive. Not only that, I fell over in the playground while I was running around with Francine. I cut both my knees, and my skirt flew up around my waist, so that everyone in the whole playground could see that I was wearing pink knickers. With bunny rabbits all over them.

Like I said, today had been a bad day.

'So how long have you been waiting to hear from the TV company *now*?' Francine persisted, as we went down the street.

'Three weeks,' I said shortly. As far as I was concerned, this telly thing had been a complete wash-out from the start. When Mum had phoned the TV company to put our names down, they'd told her that nearly five hundred other families had applied so far. *Five hundred.* The TV company had then sent us a questionnaire to fill in, asking us all about ourselves. I thought it was a waste of time, but Mum, Dad, Cindy and Jools had spent a whole week arguing about what we should or shouldn't write down on the form.

'So do you think —' Francine began again, but this time I cut her short.

'Look, France, there's no point in talking about this stupid TV thing, OK?' I snapped. 'I *told* you that about fifty million other families have applied as well, so there's just NO WAY we're going to be chosen. Now, can we talk about something else?'

'Sorry I spoke,' Francine said huffily, and we walked on in silence. After a few minutes, though, I glanced sideways at Francine's red face, and began to feel rather ashamed of myself. We hardly ever had a fight, and I hadn't meant to have a go at her like that. It was just that I was completely fed up to my back teeth with this telly thing. It was all my family had talked about for the last three weeks and I'd had enough. But that didn't mean I could take things out on Francine. After all, she *was* my best mate.

We'd reached the corner now where we had to split up and go our separate ways, and I looked hopefully at her.

'Coming over to my house tomorrow afternoon, Francine?'

Francine knew straightaway that I was trying to say sorry, and her face brightened.

'OK, see you then.'

'Bye.' I waved, and carried on down the street towards our house. I was still quite a way from the gate, when to my surprise, I saw my dad suddenly step out from behind a bush. He had a pair of shears in his hand, and he was pretending to prune the roses, but every so often he glanced anxiously up and down the street, as if he were looking for someone. I caught his eye, waved and then frowned to myself. You had to put a bomb under Dad to get him to do any gardening normally. That meant he was probably lying in wait for somebody. Me.

'Dad?' I pushed open the garden gate, an unpleasant, sick feeling settling itself firmly in the pit of my stomach.

'Oh, hello, Ally. I was waiting for you.' I was relieved to see that Dad looked OK. No one was dangerously ill then, and the cats hadn't been run over. 'What happened to your knees, love?'

'Oh, that.' I glanced down at the two plasters decorating my cut legs. 'I fell over in the playground, that's all.' Then I looked up at him curiously. 'Why're you waiting for me?'

Dad cleared his throat. He had a peculiar look on his face. Kind of both pleased and worried at the same time.

'We had a phone call from the TV company today . . .'

I stared at him.

'What?'

'They've short-listed ten families from all those who applied, and they're going to interview them before they choose one for the programme.' There was a long pause. 'We're one of the ten, love.'

My mouth dropped open in amazement.

'You're – you're joking,' I stammered.

Dad shook his head.

'No, I'm not, Ally. But what I really want to know –' his eyes searched my face '– is how you feel about it?'

I didn't say anything. I couldn't say anything because I didn't know *what* to say. I didn't even know what I felt. From being a comfortably anonymous one in five hundred families, we'd suddenly become just one in ten, bringing the TV cameras a whole lot nearer.

'Ally?'

'I – I'm not quite sure how I feel about it.' I managed to force the words out through dry lips. 'Give me a week or two to get used to it, and then I'll be OK.'

Dad looked worried.

'Er – well, the producer and the director are coming to interview us in person a little bit sooner than that . . .'

'When?'

'Tomorrow.'

'*Tomorrow*?' I repeated faintly. Things were moving a bit too fast for me. 'Why – why're they coming so soon?'

Dad shrugged.

'I don't really know. But I suppose it's so they can catch us pretty much unawares. So we haven't got time to redecorate the house, or buy a whole new wardrobe or whatever.' He reached out, and put his hands on my shoulders. 'Look, Ally, I know it's a bit of a shock, but if you really don't want to go ahead, we can still cancel —'

'No,' I cut in quickly. 'I'll be OK. When I've got used to the idea.'

Inside I was all mixed up. One bit of me was thrilled to know that my family were considered interesting enough to be on TV, but one bit of me was absolutely terrified. Yes, I was excited. But I was nervous too. I was excited, nervous, thrilled, scared and terrified all at the same time, a mixture that was making my tummy turn somersaults. But I couldn't say I didn't want to go through with it now, could I? Cindy and Jools would kill me.

'Ally, I mean it. Never mind what Cindy and Jools are going to say.' Dad always could read my mind. 'If you want us to stop right now, we will.'

'No, we can't pull out now,' I said firmly. 'I mean, it'll be an experience. And it'll be fun. Probably.'

'Well . . . OK, Ally. If you're sure.'

Dad still didn't look too convinced – and I wasn't that convinced myself. It was just the shock, that's all, I told myself firmly as we went indoors together. I'd feel better once I'd had more time to get used to the idea.

We walked straight into the Living Room from Hell. Mum was vacuuming the carpet with her hair in rollers, Jools was watching TV at full volume, and standing on a stepladder sweeping cobwebs off the ceiling with a broom at the same time, and Cindy was sitting on the sofa in her bikini, with hair-removing cream plastered all over her legs and armpits, and a mud pack crusting up her face. It was Cindy who spotted me first.

'We've been short-listed!' she shrieked at me over the noise of the vacuum-cleaner and the TV. 'Oh, blast, now I've cracked my face pack!'

'I know!' I shrieked back.

'For the TV programme!' Jools yelled at me, getting his bit in.

'I know!' I yelled back. I went over to sit on the sofa next to Cindy, wondering how on earth my family had managed to be short-listed out of nearly five hundred others. These TV people had to be either mad or desperate. Or both.

'We're on a short-list of ten!' Mum shouted at me, vacuuming the rug like crazy, and nearly sucking up one of the cats tail-first. 'They're coming to interview us tomorrow!'

'I KNOW!'

Mum turned the vacuum-cleaner off. At the same moment, Dad grabbed the remote control from Jools, and turned the TV off. There was silence for about half a second, before everybody started talking at me at once.

'Come on, you lot, give Ally a chance to catch her breath,' Dad said over the racket. 'She's only just heard the news.'

'She doesn't seem too happy about it.' Mum hurried over to me, looking concerned. 'You do want to go through with this, don't you, love?'

''Course I do,' I said weakly. 'I just can't understand why *we've* been chosen for an interview out of all those hundreds and hundreds of other families, that's all.'

'I would've thought that was obvious,' Jools said with a smug grin.

'Not to me it isn't,' I muttered.

'Oh, come on, Alice, don't be a grouch.' Cindy poked me enthusiastically in the ribs. 'We're just what they're looking for!'

'Anyway, Ally, nothing's been decided yet,' Dad said, looking at me anxiously . 'We're just going to be interviewed, that's all. Even if we're chosen, we don't have to go through with it.'

'What do you mean – not go through with it?' Cindy and Jools squealed together, but Mum glared at them.

'Your dad's right, Alice,' she said. 'This is meant to be a bit of fun, that's all. Your dad and me don't want you to get upset about it. So if you're not happy, we can ring up and cancel the interview right now.'

'Just say the word, Ally,' added my dad.

There was silence in the room now. I knew that Mum and Dad meant every word. If I wanted to pull out, they'd do it, no problem. Problem Number One was that my sister and brother were sitting and staring at me with big, pleading eyes, like puppies in a pet-shop window. And Problem Number Two was me. I felt so nervous at the thought of being filmed at home, it just wasn't true. But even if I was so nervous that my knees were knocking together, and my heart was pounding fit to bust, could I really say NO? I might never get the chance to be on TV ever again in my whole life . . . I took a deep breath, and made a decision.

'Well,' I said slowly, 'I suppose it can't do any harm just to be interviewed . . .'

'Cool!' Jools jumped up and slapped me on the back, looking relieved.

'Brilliant!' Cindy bore down on me, beaming all over her cracked face pack.

'Get away!' I yelped, ducking out of her way. 'I don't want to get covered in mud!'

'Isn't it about time you washed that stuff off

anyway?' Dad remarked, winking at me. 'You'll be chipping it off with a chisel at this rate.'

'I've got to look my best for tomorrow.' Cindy grabbed my arm, and pulled me over to the door. 'Come on, squirt. Let's go upstairs and decide what you're going to wear for the interview!'

As Cindy dragged me enthusiastically upstairs to our bedroom, I was already beginning to wonder if I'd made the right decision. If I felt so nervous now, how would I feel if the TV cameras *did* arrive? What if I ended up making an enormous fool of myself? What if I burst into tears in front of the TV camera, like I'd done on stage at Butlins? What if my voice dried up in my throat, and I couldn't speak? What if the TV camera got a shot of me sucking my thumb, like I sometimes did when I couldn't get to sleep? What if —?

'OK.' Cindy, having popped into the bathroom to wash off her mud pack, now came back into our room, smiling all over her face. 'Come on, let's get all your stuff out of the wardrobe, and check it over.'

Reluctantly I got up off the bed, and trudged across the room to the wardrobe. At this rate, I'd be happier wearing a paper bag over my head tomorrow than anything else.

'What's up?' Cindy had been looking at herself in

the mirror, and now she swung round to stare at me. 'You're really nervous about this TV thing, aren't you?'

I nodded.

'I *am* excited,' I said, biting my lip. 'But you know what? I'm really scared too . . .'

Cindy looked at me sympathetically. 'I know how you feel.'

I shook my head, and slumped back down onto my bed.

'No, you don't. You're just saying that. *You're* not nervous.'

'I *am*,' Cindy insisted. 'You don't think I want to go on TV and make a right fool of myself, do you? Of course I'm nervous in case things don't work out.'

I felt a tiny bit better.

'But you and Jools and Mum and Dad really *want* to do this,' I said slowly, 'I really want to be on TV too, but if I'm going to make a prat of myself, I'd rather not bother.'

'Look, squirt.' Cindy plumped down on the bed next to me. 'You only feel like that because you're so nervous. I mean –' she grinned at me ' – what do you want to be able to tell your grand-children in fifty years' time? Do you want to be able to tell them that you were the star of a TV programme when you were a kid, or –' she paused dramatically '– do you want to tell them that you never made it onto the telly because you chickened out at the last minute?'

Cindy surprises me sometimes. I knew what she was trying to tell me. She was trying to tell me that if I never took any risks, my life would be really dull and boring. And, I asked myself silently, did I really want to be dull, boring, mousy little Alice Mackenzie all my life? This was my big chance to prove to myself, and to everybody else, that I was different. And if I didn't take a risk, and go in for this TV thing along with everyone else, I might regret it for ever afterwards.

I just wish taking risks didn't make me feel quite so awful.

Chapter Three

The TV people *looked* like TV people. Melissa Murray, the director, was tall and slim with long dark hair and big teeth. She was wearing expensive-looking jeans, a black leather jacket and an amazing pair of large glasses with bright blue frames. Cameron Dempsey, the producer, was older. He had grey hair and a gold earring, and a sort of handkerchief tied round his neck, and they'd pulled up outside our house in a flashy black open-top sports car that had made our neighbours' eyes pop out.

'Well, it's marvellous to meet you at last,' Melissa Murray said as we all sat down in the living room. She had a posh voice, like most telly people, but she had a very friendly smile. 'Can I say first of all how well you've done just to get short-listed. We had *so* many applications, didn't we, Cameron?'

'Absolutely, Melissa.' Cameron Dempsey, who had exactly the same sort of posh voice as Melissa, nodded in agreement. 'Now, we don't have much time –' as if on cue, Melissa dived into her enormous shoulder bag, and produced a notepad and pen '– so maybe we could make a start by talking to you about some of the things you wrote down on your questionnaire . . .'

I panicked. Quietly, while no one was looking, I moved my chair a little way back, so that I was half-hidden behind Dad. Even though Melissa Murray and Cameron Dempsey seemed OK, this was the bit I wasn't looking forward to.

For the next half hour, Melissa and Cameron fired a whole load of questions at us. By the end of it they knew all about Dad's obsession with football, and his trial for the Wolves (in detail); they knew about WALLIES, and how Mum had been swindled out of the lead role in *Oklahoma!* by Marjorie Carter; they knew Cindy wanted to be a TV presenter, and how much she spent on make-up every month (a lot); and they knew all about Jools' songwriting, and his favourite band, the Dead Beats. They'd laughed when Cindy had described a typical day in the Mackenzie household, and they'd looked interested when Mum and Dad had talked about how difficult it was coping with two teenagers in the house. I don't know if Cameron and Melissa were pretending or not, but they seemed to find the whole family, including the cats, fascinating.

But what about me? No one spoke to me, or even seemed to notice I was there. Gloomily I stared down at the carpet, and bit my lip. OK, so I was used to being part of the scenery when the others were around, but I was a member of this family too, wasn't I? Had everyone forgotten that I was there?

'So what about you – er – Alice?' I jumped, as Melissa Murray glanced down at her papers to check that she'd got my name right, then leaned forward to look at me over the top of her designer glasses. 'You haven't said anything so far. Tell us all about yourself.'

I could feel myself turning scarlet from the toes up. This was it. My big chance to impress the TV people.

'Um. Well. There's – there's not much to tell,' I stammered. 'I-I go to school. C-come home. Watch telly. That kind of thing.'

I could have bitten my tongue out. Pretty impressive, I don't think. Why couldn't I string two words together without tripping myself up?

'And?' Melissa Murray stared at me encouragingly, with a friendly smile, and I felt my throat begin to seize up with terror. What did she expect me to say? That I was a child genius or something?

Luckily Dad hurried to the rescue.

'Alice is a bit shy,' he said quickly. 'Er – maybe you could tell us exactly what's involved if we get chosen?'

'Sure.' Melissa Murray lost interest in me pretty fast, and turned back to the rest of my family. I sank down into my chair, feeling annoyed and relieved both at the same time.

'Well, if you *are* chosen, you do have to be prepared for some quite major changes to your lives over the six weeks we'll be filming,' said Cameron Dempsey with a smile. I sat up, and pinned back my ears. *This* was where things started to get interesting. This was when we'd find out exactly what we were letting ourselves in for.

'What sort of changes?' asked Mum.

'Well, you'll have to be prepared to have a film crew in the house almost all the time. It would be a three-person crew – Melissa, a cameraman and our sound and light man.'

'What about you?' Jools asked.

'Me?' Cameron shrugged. 'Oh, I'm not important. I'm only the producer,' and he and Melissa both chuckled at this as if it was a huge joke. 'My work will be back at the TV studios. At the end of each week's filming, it'll be me who puts the programme together. We're calling it *Happy Families*, by the way. Obviously we can't use all the film that we shoot, so I'll have the job of deciding which bits go in, and which bits are left out.'

I glanced round. My family were sitting on the edge of their seats, their eyes shining with anticipation. As for me, I was just beginning to realise exactly what we were letting ourselves in for, and I *still* didn't know whether to feel thrilled or terrified.

'We'll be filming all week, and the first programme will go out on Friday evening,' Cameron was saying. 'Then we start filming again the next day, ready for the following Friday's programme, and so on.'

That meant six weeks of having cameras watching our every move. I gulped. Six weeks? I wasn't even sure I could cope with one *day*.

'We'll be filming mostly in the home, but if you're chosen, we'd like to shoot some outside film of you at work and at school and so on . . .'

I froze in my seat. *At school*? They had to be kidding.

'You'll be required to sign what we call a release form,' Melissa chimed in. 'That means that you agree that anything we film can be shown on air. Of course –' she winked at us '– we won't be filming in any private areas of the house such as bedrooms or bathrooms without permission!'

Everyone smiled except me. I just raised my eyes to the ceiling. Didn't the others see the catch? We'd have absolutely no say in whatever they wanted to put out on air. Even if they'd filmed something that made the Mackenzies look as weird and wacky as The Addams Family, we still wouldn't be able to stop it being shown on the telly. I glanced round the table at Mum, Dad, Cindy and Jools. Didn't they realise what was going on? Yeah, of course they did. They weren't stupid. But it wasn't enough to put them off the whole idea. It was getting to be enough to put me off though . . .

'I have to say just one more thing.' Melissa Murray tapped her pen thoughtfully against her teeth. 'If you're chosen, it's going to mean a lot of publicity. And the trouble is, everyone who appears on telly for the first time expects the viewers to love them with a capital L.'

She stared round at us.

'So what if the viewers don't take to you? How will you cope if you get some hurtful publicity in the newspapers?'

I sat and thought about that in silence for a few seconds. That was another thing I hadn't considered before. Publicity. People would be seeing us on TV, and reading about us in the newspapers, and talking about us in the street. A cold shiver ran down my spine. I'd seen TV stars getting chased by the press, every detail of their lives exposed in the newspapers. If we went ahead and did this TV thing, would we have photographers chasing us wherever we went? Would there be shock horror stories in the Sunday papers? 'Exclusive! Alice Mackenzie falls over in playground, and shows her pink knickers?'

'We'll be fine,' Cindy said confidently, tossing back her gleaming blonde hair. 'Us Mackenzies are tough!'

'Oh, I'm sure we can handle it,' Mum was saying. 'When I was in *West Side Story* with WALLIES, the local paper said I danced like a fairy elephant, and it didn't bother *me*!'

'Nope, you were fine after you'd ripped the paper into little pieces, and flushed it down the loo!' Jools put in with a wicked grin.

Melissa giggled.

'Well, if you're sure . . .' Suddenly she turned, and flashed me another warm, friendly smile. 'And what do *you* think about all this, Alice?' She put her head on one side, and looked at me shrewdly. 'I get the feeling you're not *quite* as keen on this as the rest of your family are.'

I squirmed in my chair, not knowing what to say. Dad came to my rescue yet again.

'You're quite right,' he said quietly. 'In fact, I think Alice might prefer to keep in the background as much as possible if we're chosen. Until she gets used to the cameras, at least.'

'Of course. I understand,' Melissa said sympathetically. 'Being on TV can be nerve-wracking, as well as exciting.' I felt a tiny bit better. At least *someone* understood how I was feeling. 'But, you know –' Melissa held my gaze with a steady look '– sometimes television can make shy, quiet people come out of their shells in a most dramatic way.'

I was curious. What on earth did she mean? But I didn't get the chance to find out.

'We must be going. We've got five more families to visit today.' Melissa stood up briskly. 'It's been wonderful meeting you all.'

'When we will know who's been chosen?' Cindy asked eagerly, fluttering her false eyelashes. (At least they'd stayed firmly fixed to her eyelids today.)

'We're seeing all the shortlisted families this weekend, so we'll be in touch on Monday or Tuesday of next week.' Cameron Dempsey was shaking hands all round. 'We're working to a very tight schedule here. Filming will start in the next couple of weeks or so.'

Dad, Mum, Cindy and Jools crowded round the door to see them off. I stayed in my chair, kicking at the carpet and feeling uneasy. Why had Melissa Murray looked so interested when Dad had told her how I felt about the filming? If anything, I would've thought that would put her off . . .

'We're in!' Cindy announced confidently as the two drove off in Melissa's flash car. 'They loved us!'

Mum and Dad glanced at each other, and then at me.

'Well, they *did* seem to like us,' Mum said hesitantly. 'But I'm sure the other families they're going to see have got just as good a chance.'

'It's OK, Mum,' I said, managing a smile. 'I'll cope.'

'You heard what Melissa said, anyway,' Jools pointed out kindly. 'She said it'd be OK for you to keep in the background, if you want to.'

'I know.' I was feeling even *more* confused now. Of course I wasn't planning on doing a song and dance act in front of the cameras and making myself into a TV star, but did everybody have to be quite so keen on me being kept out of the way?

Couldn't *somebody* have made just *one* pathetic attempt to persuade me to join in wholeheartedly?

'There is one thing,' I said suddenly. 'I'm not letting them film me at school. No way.'

'Don't worry, Ally,' Dad said firmly. 'You won't have to do anything you don't want to.'

'We can sort all that out when we sign the contract,' Mum added.

'*If* we're chosen,' I reminded everybody. They all seemed to be taking it for granted now that we would be. I was the only one who wasn't.

Feeling all mixed up inside, I got up and went over to the door. I'd promised to ring Francine after the interview, and tell her what had happened, and I knew that she'd probably be sitting by the phone, waiting for me to call. I needed to talk to somebody to try and sort my head out, but surprise, surprise, I didn't get the chance.

'The phone's mine!' Cindy yelled, rushing triumphantly past me down the hall. Jools, Mum and Dad immediately crowded out of the room after her, complaining loudly. I didn't bother following. I might be hopeless at maths, but I knew from experience that Cindy + telephone = a very long wait. In fact, I wouldn't have been surprised if Cindy had started phoning complete strangers from the telephone directory to tell them she was going to be a TV star. At this rate, everybody in Great Britain was going to know that the Mackenzies *might* be on the telly.

I was right. Ever seen those pictures on the telly when a famous pop singer or a film star is mobbed by a big crowd when they walk out of a hotel or something?

Well, that's exactly what happened to me on Monday morning when I got to school. When Francine and I arrived at the playground gates, we were immediately surrounded by a crowd of kids, all yelling at the top of their lungs.

'Are you gonna be on the telly, Mackenzie? Is it true?'

'Mackenzie's gonna be a film star!'

'Are the cameras going to come here?'

'Will *we* be on the telly as well?'

I looked helplessly at Francine. We couldn't move for bodies.

'Do something!' Francine hissed at me as the scrum began to move in on us.

'QUIET!' I yelled. I couldn't think of anything else to do. But it worked. The whole crowd fell silent at the sight of the school mouse, shy little Alice Mackenzie, shouting her mouth off. I was a bit stunned myself, to tell you the truth. I didn't know I had such big lungs.

'Er – thanks,' I stammered, blushing bright red all over with embarrassment. 'Um – excuse me. I need to get to class.'

Grumbling, the crowd parted to let me through.

'She isn't even on the telly yet, and she's already behaving like a film star,' I heard one girl mutter. I rolled my eyes, grabbed Francine's arm and legged it across the playground. If this was stardom, I could do without it.

'Good job you didn't tell them you're not going to let the TV cameras come and film you here,' Francine panted as we reached the safety of the school building. 'They might have killed us on the spot.'

'I know.' I bit my lip. It wasn't just my family who was dying to be on TV. It looked like everyone else in town wanted to get in on the act too. 'You know what I mean, though, don't you?' I looked pleadingly at Francine. 'Imagine Munro telling me off or something because I got all my maths wrong, and the TV people filming it! I'd die.'

'Yep, it'd be gross,' Francine agreed sympathetically. 'I'd hate it, if it was me.'

I cheered up a bit. So I wasn't totally weird after

all, not wanting the whole of my private life to be shown on a TV programme. There were some things that I didn't want to share with the viewing public, and being hopeless at maths was one of them.

'Come on.' I nudged Francine in the ribs. 'Let's go to the library or something, so that I can get some peace and quiet —'

'Alice!'

I looked round. Miss Munro, our class teacher, was hurrying down the corridor towards us.

'Yes, miss?'

'When are the film crew arriving?' Miss Munro demanded breathlessly.

I stared at her.

'Pardon, miss?'

'The film crew. For the TV programme.' Miss Munro beamed at me, and patted her blonde bob. 'I want to make sure I get my hair done in time.'

I looked at Francine. She shrugged helplessly.

'Well?' Miss Munro was gazing at me brightly. There was a hungry look in her eyes that I was fast beginning to recognise. Yep, Miss Munro had Telly Fever.

I groaned inwardly. I had to put a stop to all this before it got out of hand.

'Miss Munro, I —'

'Ah, Alice Mackenzie. Just the person I was looking for.' Before I could say anything, the headmaster, Mr Robbins, popped his bald head round the door of his study like a jack-in-the-box. 'Have I got time to have the school redecorated?'

I blinked.

'What did you say, sir?'

'It's a perfectly simple question, Alice.' Robbo bustled out of his office, carrying a pile of papers. 'Have I got time to have the school repainted before the TV cameras arrive or haven't I?'

I groaned silently again. Francine sighed.

'Shall I tell them or are you going to?' she hissed in my ear.

Shaking in my shoes, I told them. And guess what. They weren't very pleased. I tried explaining that my family hadn't even been chosen yet, and we probably wouldn't be, but it didn't make the slightest bit of difference. As far as 250 pupils, ten teachers and one headmaster were concerned (quite apart from seven dinner ladies and a caretaker), I was cheating them out of their chance of stardom with a capital S.

So I was definitely the Bad Guy.

By the end of the day, I'd had enough. Francine felt so sorry for me, she took me to the corner shop after school to buy me a Mars bar, which cheered me up a bit.

'You know, being a telly star isn't all it's cracked up to be,' Francine said thoughtfully, as we wandered home afterwards.

'You can say that again,' I sighed. 'All I'm waiting for is a phone call to say we haven't been chosen, and then I can get on with my life.'

'You'll be disappointed, though,' Francine persisted. 'I mean, you've come this far now, it'd be terrible if you weren't chosen.'

I thought about that for a moment or two.

'OK,' I admitted slowly, 'I think I *would* be a bit disappointed, but at least it'd get everyone off my back. All I've had so far is major hassles from everyone.'

'They're just jealous,' Francine said confidently. 'How many people get a chance to be on the telly?'

I suddenly felt a bit silly. Francine was right. I'd been given the chance to do something that most people would die for. So what was I moaning about? I ought to be grateful, instead of going around with a face like a wet weekend.

'I know. And I *am* excited really . . .'

Francine finished off her Mars bar, and licked her fingers.

'Maybe you'll hear something when you get home.'

She was right. I did.

As I walked up our garden path, I could hear Mum and Dad talking through the open window. I didn't mean to listen. But I heard my name mentioned a couple of times, and well, you know how it is . . .

'– and we need to be careful how we break the news to Alice,' Dad was saying. 'I think she's still a bit undecided about the whole thing.'

'Maybe we ought to speak to Alice before we tell Jools and Cindy,' Mum replied thoughtfully. 'After all, if Alice definitely doesn't want to do it, we don't have to tell the other kids that we've been chosen.'

I stood quite still on the garden path, Mum's words resounding in my head. They could only mean one thing . . .

'Oh, Dan, I still can't believe that we've been chosen out of all those hundreds of other families!' my mum went on breathlessly. 'Us – on TV! Isn't it amazing?'

My knees suddenly started trembling so much, I couldn't hold my heavy school bag any more, and I had to let it fall onto the path.

We'd been chosen for the TV programme.

Out of five hundred other families, the

Mackenzies had come out right on top.

I was so shocked, I could hardly breathe. Even after the interview, I'd never really believed that we were going to be the ones Melissa Murray and Cameron Dempsey would go for.

'I've been thinking . . .' That was Dad again. 'If Alice is really dead set against the idea, obviously we won't go ahead, but do you remember what that director woman said?'

'Melissa Murray?'

'She said that sometimes appearing on TV can be good for shy people.' There was a pause, then Dad went on: 'I worry about Alice sometimes. I think she feels a bit left out when the rest of us get going.'

'Mm, I know what you mean,' Mum agreed. 'And I think you're right. I think being on TV might be good for Alice in particular . . .'

I didn't listen any more. Instead, my heart racing, I sat down on the front doorstep, and thought about what were going to happen. For the next six weeks, there were going to be strangers in our home. Strangers with TV cameras, who were going to be filming me having my breakfast, playing with my friends, watching videos, brushing my teeth . . . I felt a shiver of excitement and sheer panic run through me.

Alice Mackenzie was going to be on TV.

Chapter Four

It was three weeks later, and it was the night before the filming of *Happy Families* was due to start. The Big Day was here at last. At eight o'clock sharp the next morning, Melissa Murray and her TV crew would arrive on our doorstep, and the Mackenzies would be making their very first appearance in front of the TV cameras . . .

No wonder then that I was lying in bed in the dark, feeling sick with nerves and excitement.

I just couldn't get to sleep. Mum had insisted that we all went to bed at 9pm, so we looked good for the cameras in the morning, but it was one o'clock already, and I was still wide awake. All I could think about was what was going to happen tomorrow . . .

The last three weeks had been hectic, to say the least. Which was good, in a way, because I hadn't had time to get any more nervous about the filming than I already was. Once I'd found out that we were definitely going to be on the TV programme (and I'd managed to get over the shock a bit), I'd thought that the camera would just arrive and start filming us immediately. But I was wrong. Television doesn't work that way.

The first thing that happened was that, a few days later, Melissa Murray and Cameron Dempsey had come back to see us to tell us how pleased they were that we were pleased that we'd been chosen. Then Melissa had turned up again a week later, along with a whole load of press photographers to take publicity pictures for the TV programme. We'd been photographed in our garden, sitting round our kitchen table, standing in the front doorway (pretty embarrassing, as all the neighbours had come out to have a good gawp), and sitting on the sofa in our living room, Mum, Dad and Cindy on the seats, and me and Jools perched uncomfortably on the arms, with the photographers standing round us, clicking away as if we were celebrities or something.

'Where will the photos be used, Melissa?' Cindy had asked.

'Oh, you'll see them all over the place,' Melissa had said confidently. 'All the TV magazines, like *Radio Times* and *TV Times*, will probably use them, and hopefully some of the national newspapers will use them to run a story about you before *Happy Families* goes out on air. We're looking to get a lot of publicity for the programme, if we can.'

Well, she'd got what she wanted. Over the last few days, there'd been pictures of us in the *Sun*, the *Daily Mirror*, the *Guardian* and the *Independent*, with headlines like 'Family to star in 'fly-on-the-wall' documentary' and we were also in *all* the TV magazines. I know we were in all of them because the whole family had gone down to W. H. Smith, and spent about an hour looking at all the magazines on the shelves. Eventually the shop assistants had got fed up with us and called the manager, but when he found out who we were, he'd insisted on shaking us all by the hand, and giving us complimentary copies of all the magazines our picture was in. We were celebrities already, and we hadn't even been on the telly yet. It was *weird*.

A few days later, Melissa had marched us all into the living room, sat us down, and given us a long lecture about all the things we could and couldn't do, now that we were about to become TV stars.

'As you know, we'll be starting filming next week –' she'd said briskly, '– so now that you've signed the contract, the one thing I have to warn you –' she'd looked round at us almost threateningly '– is not to talk to the press. If the programme takes off, you'll probably get lots of calls from the papers, pestering you for interviews. During the six weeks of filming, you must *not* give any interviews at all without checking with me first. Is that clear?' She'd swept on without waiting for an answer. 'The other really important thing is that from now on, *nothing* must be changed around the house. No new furniture, no redecoration. *Nothing*. OK?'

Mum and Dad had shot a guilty look at each other. I knew that they'd already hired someone to come in and paint the living room before filming started. Melissa had noticed the look too, and pounced straightaway.

'I'm sorry, but if you've made any arrangements, you'll have to cancel them. We can't possibly have filming disrupted if there's wet paint around, for example.' She'd stared hard at Mum and Dad until they both nodded sheepishly, and then went on, 'No changes also means that you don't alter your appearances at all. No new clothes, no new haircuts, etc.'

Then we'd *all* looked guilty. We'd been out on a shopping spree the day before.

'OK, then, no *more* new clothes,' Melissa had said with a sigh. 'And definitely no new hairstyles.

We don't want you looking completely different to the way you look in the publicity photos. Oh, and, Barbara, while I remember, the crew and I are going to need a set of house keys. Do you have a spare?'

'Er – yes,' Mum had stammered, looking as dazed as I was feeling myself. Things were starting to move a bit too fast. 'On the shelf by the front door.'

'Excellent.' Melissa had flashed us a dazzling smile. 'Right, the engineers will be arriving any moment to lay the cables, so if you could all go out for about three or four hours, that would be a big help.'

We'd all stared at her, open-mouthed.

'Sorry?' Dad had said, looking bewildered.

'You don't have enough electrical power points for all our equipment, so we need to put in some more, and we need to lay lots of extra cables for our lights,' Melissa had said airily, heading for the hall as the doorbell rang . 'Don't worry,' she'd called back over her shoulder. 'If we need to take any of your carpets up, we'll replace them carefully. Our engineers are all very experienced.'

'I hope so,' Mum had said grimly. 'Because if they ruin any of the carpets, there'll be trouble.'

'I didn't know they were going to rearrange the whole house,' Dad had said under his breath.

'*And* chuck us out while they do it,' Jools had added indignantly.

My head had been spinning at all the things Melissa had said. No new clothes without permission, phone calls from the press pestering us for interviews, strange people in the house pulling up our carpets. How on earth were we supposed to carry on living our normal, everyday lives in front of the camera, if everything around us was going to be so strange?

I rolled over onto my back, pulled the duvet up round my neck and looked at my alarm clock again. 1.15 am. Six hours and forty-five minutes to go before Melissa Murray, Nick the cameraman and Ken the sound and light man arrived, ready to start the filming. Melissa had introduced us to Nick and Ken a few days ago. She'd turned up one evening, when we were all sitting in the living room watching the TV, and she'd let herself in with the key she'd asked Mum for, as if she owned the place.

'Sorry, I'm afraid you'll have to get used to us coming and going as if we were part of the family,' she'd said apologetically, as she came into the living room with two men behind her. 'I thought I'd just pop round, and introduce you to the rest of the crew.'

One of the men was middle-aged and a bit tubby, the other was slimmer and younger, with long, dark hair. He was also quite good-looking in a moody, rock-singer kind of way. Out of the corner of my eye, I'd seen Cindy sit up in her chair.

'This is Nick Rogers, our cameraman.' Melissa indicated the dark-haired man. 'And this is Ken Wilson, our sound and light man.'

'Pleased to meet you,' Ken said cheerfully, but Nick didn't say anything. He just nodded at us.

'They're very good at their jobs, and very experienced,' Melissa went on. 'And they're both thrilled about working on this project.'

I hadn't been able to help staring at Nick. He hadn't look thrilled at all. In fact, he'd looked as if he was wishing himself a million miles away.

'We'll all get to know each other really well by the end of the six weeks,' Melissa had said with a beaming smile. 'We'll be like one 'Happy Family' ourselves!'

'That sounds nice,' Cindy had said hopefully, batting her eyelashes at Nick, who'd completely ignored her.

And now everything was ready. We'd said no to all our relatives who'd phoned up, wanting to know if they could come and stay for six weeks so that they could be in the programme too, we'd shampooed the cats, we'd spent all day yesterday cleaning and tidying the house, and all evening fighting over the bathroom (guess who won). The Mackenzies were washed, brushed and looking their best. So it was all systems go from now on . . .

Breathing hard, I lay on my back, and stared up at the ceiling, thoughts whirling round and round in my head. This was the first time for the last three weeks that I'd actually had a quiet moment to think about what was going to happen, and I was dismayed to find that I felt more terrified than ever. Excited, but terrified.

I raised myself on my elbow, and looked across the bedroom. As usual, my side was clean and tidy, and, for a change, Cindy's was too. Her side of the room was normally a complete mess, with clothes and CDs and bits of make-up scattered all over the floor, but she'd spent hours tidying it up that morning, just in case the TV cameras wanted to film it. I wondered how long she'd manage to keep it that way. For about a day, I reckoned.

Through the dark I could just see Cindy curled up in her bed by the window, snoring away as if she hadn't got a care in the world, with rollers in her hair and cream all over her face. After we'd come to bed, we'd talked for a couple of hours about the TV programme, and what was going to happen tomorrow, and that had made me feel more wide awake than ever. Wearily I flopped back down onto my pillow. If I didn't get to sleep soon, I was going to make my first appearance in front of the camera looking like a panda, with big black circles under my eyes. Great.

I snuggled down under the duvet, and started counting sheep. But by the time I got to five, the sheep had turned into Melissa Murrays grinning at me as they jumped over the fence. I groaned, and buried my head in my pillow, but the sound of our bedroom door being pushed open made me look up. It was Dad.

'All right, Ally?' He tiptoed over to me. 'I just thought I'd check up on you. See how you are.'

'You mean you guessed I wouldn't be asleep yet.' I sat up in bed and hugged my knees. 'How did you know?'

'Well, why do you think I'm still awake myself?' Dad grinned at me as he perched on the edge of the bed. 'I've been counting sheep till they're coming out of my ears.'

'Me too,' I said with a giggle, 'Only they turned into Melissa Murrays instead!'

We both started laughing under our breath, trying not to wake Cindy up.

'I haven't been this nervous since my trial for the Wolves,' Dad said, shaking his head.

'I haven't been this nervous since —' I paused, then started to giggle again. 'I've *never* been this nervous before! Dad, I'm terrified!'

We both shook silently with laughter. I don't know what was so funny about being so nervous. But we just couldn't stop laughing.

'I know what you mean.' Dad wiped his eyes. 'I'm terrified too.'

'You know what I'm scared of most?' I looked up at him. 'Making a complete fool of myself.'

'Oh, we all feel like that, Ally.' Dad leaned over, and smoothed my hair off my face. 'There isn't one of us who isn't feeling scared and nervous about tomorrow, just like you.'

A blissfully loud snore from Cindy echoed across the room just then, and we both started giggling again.

''Night, love.' Dad stood up, and winked at me. 'Try and get some sleep.'

'OK. 'Night.'

After Dad had gone, I curled up under the duvet, feeling better. Dad was right. Everybody was nervous about tomorrow, not just me. I yawned, and rubbed my eyes. At long last, I could feel myself drifting off into sleep . . .

'Alice!' Only a few minutes after I'd fallen asleep, I was being shaken awake.

'Go 'way!' I groaned, hiding my face in my pillow. 'It's not morning yet!'

'Of course it's morning!' Cindy grabbed my duvet, and yanked it off me. 'It's eight o'clock, time to start the filming! Melissa and the crew have just arrived!'

That woke me up.

'What!' I sat bolt upright, and rubbed my eyes. Sunlight was streaming in through the windows, and my alarm clock said 8.03.

'I've been up since six!' Cindy was standing in front of the mirror, brushing her hair. 'I wanted to wake you up earlier, but Dad said not to.' She spun round on her heel, and paraded around the bedroom in front of me. 'Well, what d' you think?'

I blinked. She was wearing a velvet top, a mini-skirt and long, silver earrings. Not exactly the sort of outfit you expect to see someone wearing at the breakfast table. But she looked good.

'You look great.' I yawned and stretched, trying to wake myself up. I felt as if I'd only had five minutes sleep, and I'd have given anything to be able to snuggle back down under my duvet. But how could I? There was a TV camera awaiting my appearance downstairs. I felt my tummy twist itself into a knot, and I gulped.

Cindy was slinking over to the door on her four-inch heels.

'God, I'm so nervous!' she muttered. 'I'm going down now –' she swung round to look at me '– unless you want me to wait for you?'

'No, you go on,' I said quickly. I wasn't ready to go down just yet.

'OK.' Cindy disappeared, and I could hear her heels clacking down the stairs. I heard her hurrying down the hall, open the kitchen door, and then – silence.

Well, I couldn't put it off much longer, I told myself firmly. I had to do it some time.

I had to go downstairs, face the camera and be filmed.

Chapter Five

I pushed back the duvet, and climbed slowly out of bed. I had to climb out slowly, because my legs were shaking like two blancmanges. What *had* the Mackenzie family got themselves into here?

I sat on the carpet, and considered my options. As far as I could see, there were only two things I could do.

1) Go downstairs and be filmed.

2) Stay in bed (and it was quite possible that Melissa Murray, Nick the cameraman and Ken the sound and light man would all troop upstairs, and film me in my Garfield pyjamas anyway).

I decided to go downstairs. In any case, I wanted to find out what was going on down there.

I tiptoed out onto the landing and listened hard, but I couldn't hear much except a murmur of voices coming from the kitchen. On my way to the bathroom, I checked Mum and Dad's room, and Jools's too. No one there. That meant that everyone was already downstairs, strutting their stuff for the camera. I was dying to know what was happening, but the thought of going to find out, all on my own, made me feel sick. Why hadn't I gone down with Cindy, I asked myself with a silent groan.

I spent ages in the bathroom, dawdling about and cleaning my teeth five times, but in the end I had to admit defeat. As slowly as possible, I went back to my bedroom, put on a new skirt and tee-shirt that Mum had bought me, and looked critically at myself in the mirror.

I was combing my hair, and wondering if filming had actually started or if they were all sitting there waiting for me to make an appearance, when I heard footsteps on the stairs. I froze, clutching my comb in my hand. Who was it? Was it the film crew sneaking upstairs to catch a secret shot of me with my hair looking like a bird's nest gone wild?

There was a knock at the door.

'Who – who is it?' I stammered faintly.

'It's me, Ally.' Dad's head appeared round the door, and I almost collapsed with relief. 'Thought you might need a bit of moral support.'

'What's going on down there?' I asked curiously. 'Have they started filming yet?'

'Yep, we're all sitting round having breakfast.' Dad smiled reassuringly at me. 'Come on, love. You can't put it off for ever.'

Dad was right. Anyway, now that he'd come to fetch me, I didn't feel so nervous. At least now I had somebody to hide behind when I made my Grand Entrance into the kitchen.

We went downstairs together, my heart pounding fearfully. The kitchen door was shut, and as I stood and waited for Dad to push it open, I hoped I'd be able to scuttle safely to my seat without anyone noticing me, while I sussed out exactly what was happening.

Some hope.

As soon as I set foot in the kitchen, everyone who was in there swung round to look at me. Mum, Cindy and Jools were sitting stiffly and primly at the breakfast table, Melissa was standing by the cooker, Ken had a microphone on a long stick held over the table and Nick was pointing his camera straight at me. I was being filmed.

I felt myself turn purple with embarrassment from my toes upwards. Stupidly, I froze in the doorway as if my legs had turned to stone, which gave Nick plenty of time to focus in on my terrified face.

'Good morning, Alice, dear,' Mum said brightly in her posh voice, the one she uses when she answers the phone. 'Come and sit down and have some breakfast.'

'Good morning, Alice,' chorused Cindy and Jools just as brightly.

If I hadn't been so nervous, I would've burst out laughing. This was the Mackenzies like I'd never seen them before. The all-new, improved TV version.

I was just bracing myself to walk as normally as possible over to my chair, when the doorbell rang.

'I'll go,' I said in a strangled voice. Anything to get away from the horrible, unblinking eye of Nick's camera. I turned and hurried down the hallway, almost tripping over the rug in my haste to get away. Was I going to be this nervous every single morning for the next six weeks, I asked myself anxiously. I just couldn't believe what I'd gone and let myself in for.

'Morning, love.' The postman was beaming at me from the doorstep, and holding out a couple of letters. 'Here's your post.'

I looked at him, bewildered.

'Why didn't you push it through the letterbox like you usually do?'

'Oh, it's the personal touch.' The postman was doing strange things with his head. He was craning his neck from one side to the other as if he was in pain or something. 'Got to keep my customers happy.'

'Have you got a bad neck?' I asked him politely.

'What? Oh, no.' The postman was squinting over my shoulder towards the kitchen. 'That TV crew arrived yet?'

Now I got it. I should've realised from that look on his face. Another victim of Telly Fever.

'Yes, they have, thank you,' I said hurriedly, beginning to push the door to.

The postman put out his hand to stop me.

'Thought they might like to include a few shots of me delivering your post,' he said eagerly. 'You know, add a bit of local flavour to the programme.'

'Um – I don't know,' I muttered, feeling hot all over with embarrassment. 'Sorry. I've got to go.'

I went back into the kitchen, but this time I avoided looking at Nick and his camera. Instead I scuttled into an empty seat next to Dad, gave him the post and made myself as small as possible.

'Why, thank you, my dear,' said Dad in a BBC newsreader kind of voice. I groaned inwardly.

'Can I get you something, Alice?' asked Cindy politely. 'Tea, coffee, juice?'

I was beginning to feel as if I'd walked in on somebody else's family by mistake. I glanced over at Melissa Murray, but she didn't look annoyed or angry, even though this new, improved version of the Mackenzie family couldn't have been a bit what she expected.

'Juice, please,' I muttered, horribly conscious of Ken's microphone hovering over the table.

'And what about you, Jools?' Cindy went on as she daintily poured me a glass of orange from the cut-glass jug on the table. 'Can I get you anything?'

'I'll have some juice too, thank you, Cindy,' said Jools primly.

This was too much. Everyone was acting as if we were in a play about the most perfect family in the world or something. I took the bowl of cornflakes Mum offered me, and angrily swallowed a large mouthful. One went down the wrong way, and I started to choke.

'Ally?' Dad turned to me in alarm. I could only splutter in reply.

'What's the matter?' Mum leapt up from her seat. 'She's choking, Dan! Do something!'

My eyes were watering, and I couldn't breathe. And all the time I was choking, I was conscious of Nick pointing the camera at me. If I choked to death right here on the spot, would they just stand there and film it? What a great opening scene for the first programme.

'Here, have some water.' Cindy thrust a glass

into my hand, as Dad slapped me hard on the back a few times. All at once my aching throat started to clear.

'You all right, squirt?' Jools asked, looking concerned.

'I'm – fine,' I gasped. Except for the thought that I was going to end up on TV in a few days' time, coughing my guts out in front of the whole nation.

'OK, Nick, cut.' Melissa's voice startled me. I'd almost forgotten she was there. 'If Alice is OK, I'd just like to make a few comments about what's happened so far this morning.'

We all looked expectantly at her.

'I just wanted to say that you're doing fine at the moment. Except –' she paused '– you're all trying a teeny weeny bit too hard. We probably won't use any of the stuff we've shot so far –' I cheered up instantly. So the viewing public *wasn't* going to see exclusive pictures of me choking to death on a corn flake '– because we want you to get used to the camera being around first. Don't try too hard to forget about us being here. You'll find it'll happen naturally after a while.' She turned to Nick. 'Okay, let's carry on.'

Immediately Mum, Dad, Cindy, Jools, yes, and me too, sat up in our chairs and fixed the same bright smiles to our faces. It was just so hard *not* to be artificial, when you had a camera pointing straight at you all the time.

'More toast, anyone?' Mum asked in her posh voice.

'Yes, please, Mum – I mean, Mother,' Cindy corrected herself hastily. 'Pass the butter please, Jools – AAARGH!'

We all leapt a mile at Cindy's screech, including Melissa Murray, and Nick nearly dropped his camera on Dad's head.

'What's the matter, love?' gasped Mum in her normal voice.

'I saw someone at the window looking in!' Cindy squealed. 'A Peeping Tom!'

We all stood up, and looked out of the kitchen window. A youngish man in blue overalls was standing outside on the patio, waving at us. He had a cloth in one hand, and a bucket in the other.

'That's not a Peeping Tom – it's Dave the window cleaner,' Mum said through gritted teeth, waving back at him. 'What on earth is he doing here? He only cleaned the windows last week.'

'Go out and ask him nicely to move, will you, Ken?' Melissa said calmly.

'Be a pleasure,' Ken said with a cheeky grin. He went out through the back door, and we watched him talking to Dave, the two of them waving their arms about as if they were in a silent film.

I looked at Melissa Murray, thinking that she might be annoyed, but she wasn't.

'Don't worry.' She turned to smile at us all. 'These things always happen when you're filming real-life situations.'

By the time we'd managed to get rid of Dave the star-struck window-cleaner, the toast had gone cold, and Dad had to make some more. This had to be just about the longest breakfast ever. Not only that, we had twelve phone calls asking us how the filming was going, and Mrs Jackson from next door came round to borrow a cup of sugar. Along with her husband, three kids, the family dog and an auntie who was staying with them.

By the end of breakfast, I was exhausted.

It was my turn to do the washing-up, but luckily for me, Cindy and Jools were arguing politely over which one of them should do it.

'Oh, I'll do it, Jools. I don't mind. Really.'

'No, Cindy, let me.'

I could hardly stop myself from laughing. Cindy and Jools being so polite to each other (for so long) was unheard of.

'Time we made a start on the shopping, Alice.' Mum smiled across the table at me. 'Shall we go?'

A shiver of excitement ran down my spine. Mum and I always went to the supermarket together on Saturday morning, but today was going to be special. Melissa Murray had already told us that she wanted to go with us, and film us doing our shopping.

'Right, I'll just get my coat,' Dad said heartily.

Mum and I looked at each other. Usually it takes a very hard kick in the seat of his pants to get Dad to go to the supermarket.

'You're coming with us then, are you, Dan?' Mum asked.

'Certainly,' said Dad in his newsreader voice.

'I'm coming too,' Cindy called from the sink, where she was finishing the washing-up.

'And me,' said Jools, who was drying.

I grinned to myself. Looked like nobody could resist the chance to show off in front of the cameras, even at the boring old supermarket! I glanced quickly over at Melissa to see if she looked annoyed, but she still didn't look at all fazed. All she said was, 'OK, Nick, let's get some shots of them getting into the car, and so on. I've already cleared things with the supermarket manager.'

We all got our coats and went out of the front door, with Nick filming our every move. To my surprise, though, I realised that I was already starting to get used to him being there, and to having a camera pointing in our direction. It was amazing how quickly you began to forget that you were being filmed all the time. Maybe the next six weeks wasn't going to be so nerve-wracking after all, I thought to myself quite cheerfully as I pulled on my denim jacket.

But as soon as we set foot outside, I felt embarrassed all over again. In the couple of minutes or so it took us to come out of the house, down our garden path and get into the car, just about everybody in the whole street zoomed out of their houses to goggle at us. Some people pretended to be pulling up weeds or bringing in their milk, but most just stood and stared with their mouths open. Feeling like an animal in a zoo, I looked sheepish, and tried to hide behind Dad.

'Alice, get in shot, please,' Nick said gruffly, and I turned bright red.

The supermarket was an experience. Everybody, but everybody, was staring at us as we all trooped in, from the other shoppers to the people on the check-out desks. Cindy pranced along in front, enjoying every minute of the attention, while I slid back behind Dad, and hoped Nick wouldn't notice this time.

'Look at Cindy hogging the camera,' Jools whispered crossly in my ear. 'The silly cow thinks she's Michelle Pfeiffer.'

'You're just jealous!' I hissed back. But secretly I was jealous too. Cindy had said that she was nervous, but she certainly didn't look it. I wished I could be as cool as she was, with so many people gawping at us as if we had three heads or something.

We all went round the supermarket with Mum pushing the trolley, Dad walking behind her, me skulking behind Dad and Cindy and Jools trying to elbow their way into the best position in front of Nick's camera. Melissa ran alongside us, staying out of shot, but keeping a sharp eye on what was going on, and asking goggle-eyed shoppers to move their trolleys out of the way. After a little while, once I'd got used to all the attention, I have to admit I began to feel pretty important.

The shopping usually takes Mum and me forty minutes, but today it took about two hours, because everyone wanted to have a Major Discussion about every item that went into the trolley (while they all smiled brightly into Nick's camera, and made sure he was filming their best profile). But I couldn't help smiling to myself when I noticed how the masks, including mine, were starting to slip already.

Although everyone was still showing off like mad for the camera, they were forgetting to talk in their posh voices every now and then. At one point, I completely forgot about Nick, and started chatting to Dad about football. It took me about five minutes to realise that Nick was filming, and then I turned bright red, and stopped in the middle of a sentence. Not only that, Cindy and Jools were teetering on the verge of an argument over which brand of pizza they wanted, and only stopped themselves when they remembered that they were being filmed. Mum, too, was just about to tell Dad off for staring longingly at the cigarette kiosk, when she caught Nick's camera pointed at her, and bit her tongue. Melissa had been right when she'd said we'd all forget about the camera eventually, I thought with a grin. It wouldn't be long now before the *real* Mackenzies surfaced again.

It wasn't. It happened when we finally made it out of the supermarket and back to the car park.

'I think I'll make my special pasta for tea tonight,' Mum said brightly as she and Dad heaved bulging carrier bags into the back of the car. 'Is that OK with everybody?'

'Don't bother making anything for me, Mum,' Cindy said, leaning against the car and studying her nails. 'I'm going out tonight.'

'Oh, no you're not,' Dad growled in his normal voice, which was a bit of a shock after his newsreader mode. 'You're grounded after last weekend, madam.'

The bright smile on Cindy's face was instantly replaced by a familiar pout.

'But, Dad —'

'No buts, Cindy. You heard what your father said.' Mum had completely dropped her telephone voice too now, as if she'd suddenly forgotten all about the TV crew, who were standing a little way off. 'If you're not going to come home until four o'clock in the morning and worry us sick, what do you expect?'

'I'm old enough to stay out late if I want to!' Cindy retorted furiously. 'Anyway, I *told* you, Rick's car broke down —'

'Well, why didn't you phone us?' Dad asked reasonably. 'Then your mum and I wouldn't have had to sit there worrying.'

I looked at Cindy. I hadn't had any sleep that night either, waiting for her to come back, and wondering where she was. I knew how worried Mum and Dad had been too. Dad had smoked like a chimney all night, and I don't think Mum had any fingernails left.

'What about when Jools stayed out till three

o'clock a couple of weeks ago?' Cindy demanded hotly, 'He wasn't grounded, was he? Oh, no, just because I'm a *girl* —'

'It's got nothing to do with that,' Mum snapped. 'At least Jools had the sense to phone us, and explain why he was going to be late —'

'Yeah, so there, airhead!' Jools chimed in smugly.

Cindy turned on him, and gave him a shove.

'Who asked *you* to stick your big fat nose in?' she yelled.

Everyone was arguing now. A real, full-scale Mackenzie row. And everyone seemed to have forgotten about the camera riveted on us, except me. I peered round Dad's arm, and watched what was going on. Melissa Murray was standing absolutely still, a look of satisfaction on her face, lapping up what was being played out before her very eyes. Now she was getting exactly what she wanted. Raw, uncut family life. Family life on the front line.

And you know what? I just couldn't *wait* to see the first programme.

Chapter Six

By the time Friday came round, (the day that the first part of *Happy Families* was being shown), I was wondering what on earth I'd been so nervous about. It was amazing just how quickly everybody, including me, had got used to the camera being around. After a day or two of being filmed, you started to forget that the camera was there, however much you tried to carry on being on your best behaviour. Not that I'd gone and done anything wild and outrageous (I never do), but I hadn't really tried to stay in the background much either. After all the worrying I'd done beforehand, I actually wasn't finding it difficult to get on with my normal everyday life. I got up, went to school, came home, watched TV and did all the things I always did. Nothing had really changed that much; and when I remembered how nervous I'd been before filming started, I couldn't understand why I'd got so steamed up.

'Now we want to get your reactions to the first show on film.' Melissa was bustling about, telling us where to sit, and rearranging the living-room furniture. 'Nick, if you stand over here, you should be able to get them all in shot at the same time. Ken, we want to be able to hear their comments about the programme, so check the sound levels, would you?'

Nick moved silently into position where Melissa had indicated. He still hadn't said much to any of us, not even to Cindy, who'd got fed up with fluttering her eyelashes at him. Maybe that was why we'd got used to having him and his camera around so quickly. He kind of blended into the wallpaper. Not like Ken, who was whistling loudly through his teeth as he checked the mikes.

'Oh, I just can't wait to see myself on the telly!' Cindy announced enthusiastically, elbowing Jools skilfully out of the way in the rush for the most comfy armchair. 'Only two minutes to go!'

'I watched the first programme back at the studios this afternoon,' Melissa said with a satisfied smile, 'And it's excellent. After that first morning, you've all settled in and taken to the camera remarkably well. Thanks for all your hard work, and for being so patient.'

'Come and sit by me, Ally.' Dad patted the sofa next to him. 'Looking forward to it?'

'You bet!' I said eagerly, curling up beside him. I was even looking forward to the next five weeks of filming, now that I wasn't quite so nervous.

'Quick, it's time!' Mum said breathlessly, as the ads finished. 'Dan, start the video!'

My dad grabbed the remote control and pressed the 'record' button as the TV announcer said: 'And now for the first programme in a new series. What is life really like for an ordinary family living in Britain in the 1990s?'

'*Ordinary*?' Cindy sniffed in disgust, but we all shushed her, even Nick.

'Let's find out by taking a fly-on-the-wall look at a typical British family in *Happy Families*.'

I swallowed hard as the programme's theme tune began. Suddenly I felt as if I was going to be sick with excitement right there and then, (and wouldn't Melissa have loved getting *that* on film). In just a very few seconds I was going to be seeing myself and everybody else on screen for the very first time.

The words 'Happy Families' came up in white on a black background. Then that slowly faded away, and – there we were, on the telly. Sitting on the sofa and staring into the camera. Melissa had made us pose like a Victorian family in one of those faded old photographs – Mum, me and

Cindy sitting down, and Dad and Jools standing behind. I goggled. I was so stunned, I couldn't say a word.

'This is the Mackenzie family,' said the actor who was doing the voice-over. 'Daniel Mackenzie, aged 40, is a bus driver.' The camera moved across, and suddenly Dad was in close-up on the screen.

'Blimey, I don't really look that old, do I?' Dad sat forward on the edge of the sofa, and stared at his own face on the TV. 'I look about ninety!'

'His wife Barbara, aged 38, is a waitress –' the voice went on.

The camera moved again, and this time Mum's face filled the screen.

'Oh, my God!' Mum screamed. 'I look horrible – all old and wrinkly!'

We all giggled. We couldn't help it. Everybody *did* look really different.

'Their elder daughter Cindy is fifteen, and still at school . . .'

Then Cindy was on-screen, looking a bit nervous, but still lovely as she smiled into the camera. She looked almost better on TV than she did in real life.

'It's me!' Cindy squealed joyously. 'It's really, really me!'

'Next is Julian, aged fourteen,' the voice went on.

'JULIAN?' Jools screeched, outraged, as his face filled the screen – or rather, his shades did. Melissa had tried to persuade him to take them off, but he'd refused point-blank. I began to giggle, and then it suddenly hit me.

I was next.

'And finally there is eleven-year-old Alice,' the voice continued. I turned the colour of an over-ripe tomato as the camera zoomed towards me for a close-up. It was the weirdest feeling. There I was, sitting in my own living room, looking at *my* face on the TV.

'I look really childish!' I said, amazed.

'Well, you *are* a child, love!' Mum pointed out.

'SSSHHH!' hissed the others, as the programme proper began. It started off with some film of us at breakfast; not the film they'd shot that first day when everybody had been acting like the Royal Family, but some they'd taken later in the week, when everyone had calmed down a bit, and got more used to the camera. There were Cindy and Jools flicking bits of butter at each other, my mum burning the toast, my dad hiding behind his morning paper, having a fag – and me, sitting in my usual place, writing in my Top Secret Notebook.

The bits I thought were most interesting were what I hadn't actually seen – the film of Mum and Dad at work, and of Cindy and Jools at school. I'd seen Dad driving his bus loads of times before, of course, but somehow I'd never realised just how good at his job he was. There was some film of him dealing with a really irritating passenger, who said he'd been charged the wrong fare. Dad stayed super-calm, even when the man was yelling at him, and finally got it all sorted out.

'Dad, you were excellent!' said Jools admiringly. 'I'd have smacked him one, if it'd been me.'

Dad winked at him.

'I would've done if the camera hadn't been there!'

Next there was some film of Mum at the Pizza Palace where she waitresses. As we watched her being filmed zooming round all the tables, carrying about eight large pizza plates at a time, I began to feel a bit guilty. I'd never realised before just how hard Mum worked. Maybe I ought to do more around the house in future . . .

The film of Cindy and Jools at school was even more eye-opening. I sort of knew vaguely that Cindy did OK at school, and that she wasn't stupid or anything, (even though she sometimes pretended to be a bit of a dumb blonde), but I was amazed to see just how many of the top classes she was in. And it was also a bit of a shock to see Jools being filmed speaking at a school debate - and doing pretty well too. It was fascinating. It was like seeing my family in a whole new light.

There were quite a few rows shown too. There was the argument outside the supermarket for one, and several other disagreements between Mum, Dad and Cindy about what time she was supposed to get home, with Jools sticking his nose in, and stirring things up. There was a row between Jools and Dad about the state of Jools's bedroom, and Mum having a go at Cindy about her sneakily turning up her school skirt four inches. There were also several slanging matches between Jools and Cindy, and one that almost ended in a punch-up. It was all pretty fascinating stuff.

'Oh, don't miss this bit!' Cindy sat up in her chair and started giggling. 'This is so funny!'

On the TV Cindy and Jools were standing on the landing, arguing. Jools was asking Cindy if she'd been nicking his CDs again, because he couldn't find the one he wanted to play. Cindy said she hadn't seen his stupid CD. But when Jools had stomped off downstairs to look for it, the film showed Cindy sneak into her bedroom, come out with the missing CD, tiptoe into Jools's room and put it back in the empty CD case. While all this was being shown on screen, Cindy was squealing with laughter.

'Oh, ha ha, very funny,' Jools muttered, shooting her a poisonous look.

After that, there was an interview with Mum and Dad about the problems of bringing up teenagers in the Nineties. And then suddenly the music was starting again, and the credits were rolling. The first programme was already over.

Everyone burst out talking at once. Everyone except me. I sat on the sofa, silent and alone. I was stunned.

In the whole half hour of the programme, I'd been on screen for about two minutes.

And that was all.

In fact, if it came to a count, the cats had probably been on screen more than I had.

I could hardly believe it. If I'd blinked, I would've missed me.

A huge lump was slowly forming in my throat and I had to swallow hard to hold back a sob. But it served me right, anyway, I told myself bitterly. If I'd thought about it a bit more, I would have realised that there was no chance I was going to be in the programme much anyway. After all, I *was* the quietest and most boring member of the Mackenzie family, wasn't I? It was no wonder then that the crew hadn't thought that I was interesting enough to film . . . And even if I hadn't already admitted the fact that I *was* so boring to myself, my non-appearance in the programme would've rammed it cruelly home.

So why was I so upset? I was upset because I felt like an outsider in my own family. I'd felt like an outsider before, but this was different. This TV programme had made it sort of – *official.*

'Right, I'm going up to my room,' Jools muttered, heading over to the door. Come to think of it, he didn't look much happier than I did. 'I've got homework to do.'

'Me too,' I mumbled, sliding off the sofa. Nobody took any notice. Dad was lighting a cigarette to steady his nerves, Mum was telling him to put it out, and announcing that she was going on a strict diet, and Melissa was telling Cindy how photogenic she was, and how she could be a model if she wanted to. Cindy looked just like a cat who'd had several large bowls of cream.

Outside in the hallway, Jools grabbed my arm.

'Can you believe that?' he hissed at me.

'What?' I asked, bewildered.

'Cindy, of course!' Jools looked hurt as well as

bitterly angry. 'She just hogged the camera from start to finish – and she made me look a right prat over that CD she nicked!'

I shrugged.

'Oh, come on, you two do things like that to each other all the time, and worse –'

'Yeah, but not in front of twelve million viewers!' Jools snapped. 'Right, she's for it now! I'll show her . . .'

'What're you going to do?' I asked, alarmed by the venom in his voice. But Jools didn't answer me. He just grabbed his leather jacket, and stalked out of the house, slamming the door behind him.

I stared after him, biting my lip. Just for a second there it had sounded as if Jools hated – really hated – Cindy . . . Sure, they rowed a lot, and they said they hated each other almost every day, but I knew they didn't mean it.

This time, though, I wasn't so sure . . .

And I didn't like it.

'Alice! Look at this – we're all over the newspapers!'

When I went down to breakfast the next morning, the kitchen was in an uproar. Melissa, Mum, Dad and Cindy were knee-deep in newspapers, chattering excitedly, while Nick and Ken were setting up their equipment.

'Looks like you're famous, kid!' Ken said with a wink. Nick didn't say anything at all, as usual.

'Look!' Cindy thrust a newspaper under my nose. It was folded open at the TV pages, and there was an article headed 'Joanne Carter's Review of Last Night's TV – *Happy Families* with the Mackenzies.'

Eagerly I took the paper, and read the article. The journalist had written:

> 'The new six-part series *Happy Families* got off to a flying start last night, as we were introduced to the Mackenzie family from Wolverhampton. The Mackenzies were chosen from five hundred other families to star in this fly-on-the-wall documentary series, and, even on this first showing, it's easy to see why. They seem amusing, talented and bright, and they have a real star in gorgeous teenage daughter Cindy . . .'

I skimmed quickly through the rest of the article. Most of it was about Cindy. Mum and Dad also came out of it well, as 'caring' parents, and Jools was mentioned several times. I wasn't.

'There's obviously a lot of interest in the programme,' Melissa said with a satisfied smile, 'Especially in Cindy' – Cindy tossed her hair back, and preened herself – 'so maybe we should think about publicising her a bit more. We could sort out an interview and a fashion shoot for one of the teen magazines, perhaps.'

'OK,' Cindy said eagerly.

Melissa smiled at her, and picked up her pen and notepad.

'I'll write that down so I don't forget. Come on, Nick, let's get started then. I'd like to get a few shots of their reactions as they look at the reviews. I think it would be good if we had Dan walking in with the papers under his arm as if he's just been to the shop to buy them, and they all grab them off him.'

Staying out of sight behind Dad, I quickly picked up the other papers, and looked at all the TV pages. Most of them had reviewed the show, and I began to feel quite sick, as I realised that I wasn't mentioned in a single one of them. Oh, sorry, yes, I was mentioned once. The writer said I was nine years old, and my name was Alison.

Biting my lip, I dropped the paper back onto the kitchen table. It was official, then. I definitely *was* the most boring and untalented member of the Mackenzie family, and that was that.

Swallowing hard to clear the lump in my throat, I glanced up to find Dad staring at me with a concerned look on his face. I forced a smile.

'All right, love?' he asked me quietly.

I didn't get a chance to reply. At that moment the kitchen door opened, and Jools came in. We all looked up, and there was a collective gasp of horror.

'Jools!' Mum said in a faint voice. 'What – what have you done to your *hair*?'

We couldn't take our eyes off him. Last night Jools's hair had been brown.

Today it was purple.

Bright purple.

Fluorescent aubergine, to be exact.

Jools grinned jauntily into Nick's camera, and ran his hand through his purple locks.

'Like it?' he asked.

'Like it?' Dad pushed his chair back violently, his face turning almost the same shade of purple. 'LIKE IT? I'll give you like it, my lad!'

'Dan, calm down!' Mum leapt to her feet too. 'He can wash it out – it's not permanent.' She looked pleadingly at Jools. 'It's not permanent, is it, love?'

'Yep,' said Jools calmly.

Nick's camera was super-glued to the major row that immediately erupted with Jools yelling that he was just trying to assert his individuality, Dad threatening to shave Jools's head himself, and Mum trying desperately to calm them both down. Melissa stood silently by, watching with avid interest.

'I don't believe it!' Cindy hissed furiously. Nobody was taking the slightest bit of notice of her, so she turned to me. 'The little rat!'

'What?' I was more interested in watching the row going on at the other end of the kitchen.

'Jools, that's what!' Cindy glared at me. 'If he thinks he can get away with this, he can think again!'

'What d'you mean?' I asked, puzzled.

'He's done this deliberately to try and make himself the star of the next programme!' Cindy hissed in my ear. 'Well, he won't get one over on me that easily!'

'Wait a minute.' I said, alarmed. I could see this turning into a major feud over the next five weeks. 'He's only done it because he was upset about that CD stunt you pulled on last night's programme.'

For a second or two I thought Cindy looked a bit ashamed of herself. But it didn't last. Her eyes narrowed.

'He's going to wish he'd never been born!' she snapped, and flounced out of the kitchen.

I watched her go. Then I glanced over at Jools and Dad, who were still yelling at each other, and poor old Mum running around in circles trying to calm them down.

Did I say I was looking forward to the next five weeks?

I was beginning to wish that television had never been invented.

Chapter Seven

It was Wednesday, four days after the Jools' Purple Hair Shock Horror Affair. School had just finished, but instead of going straight home I'd headed over to the local park, and wandered about aimlessly for a bit on my own. If Francine hadn't had to go to the dentist with her mum, she'd have come and wandered aimlessly with me, but I didn't mind being on my own. Anything was better than going home just at the moment . . .

There'd been big rows all weekend because of the colour of Jools's hair, and I mean big. Dad was furious, Mum was tearful, Jools was unconcerned (or at least he pretended to be), and Cindy was sulking. Nick had filmed every single one of the rows for Friday's programme, and I think Melissa was well pleased with the way things were going. I didn't blame her, really. After all, it wouldn't have made for a very interesting programme if we'd all sat around being mega-polite to each other like we did on the very first day. But I was beginning to feel as if my whole family was falling to bits around me.

Jools had gone off to school on Monday morning as normal, but with purple hair. He had stayed in school for precisely thirty seconds. Then the headmistress, Mrs Downey, had marched him back home, and issued A Warning. Unless Julian's hair was returned to its normal colour immediately, he was suspended.

Mrs Downey had put Mum's back right up. With an 'I know my rights' look on her face, Mum had told her that, whatever colour Jools's hair was, he ought to be allowed to go to school. After all, having purple hair didn't affect the way your brain worked.

Mrs Downey had retorted that there was obviously something wrong with Julian's brain anyway if he wanted to go around looking like a fluorescent aubergine, and besides, the only official hair colours recognised by the school were black, blonde, brunette and ginger. Either Jools washed the colour out, or *he* was out.

When Dad discovered that Jools had been suspended, he'd practically foamed at the mouth, and said the purple hair had to go, even if he had to hold Jools's head under the tap himself. Mum had argued that it shouldn't matter if Jools had purple hair with green stripes, he still had the right to a decent education. So now Mum and Dad are rowing all the time (when they're speaking to each other, that is).

Jools didn't seem to care that much. As far as I could see, he'd spent the last few days going into town, and sitting in McDonalds all day. Melissa, Ken and Nick were following him around like shadows, and filming his every move, totally ignoring the rest of us. So Cindy had been feeling left out and neglected, which meant the rest of us were suffering . . .

Can you blame me for not wanting to go straight home?

I carried on wandering through the park, feeling worried. This week had been bad already, and it was only Wednesday. Still two more days to go before the second programme in the series went out on air. Would Jools get rid of his purple hairdo? Would Cindy get her nose pierced, like she'd been threatening to? Would Mum and Dad ever speak to each other again? Would the Mackenzie family survive another four weeks of filming?

I glanced round. It was a grey, miserable day with a blank, cloud-filled sky overhead, and a cold chill in the air, which exactly matched my mood.

There were hardly any other people about, except for some teenage boys with a puppy in the distance. With a sigh, I sat down on a hard wooden bench near the gate, trying to find the energy to go home. I wasn't sure I could stand another evening of Mum, Dad and Jools arguing about purple hair, while Nick, Melissa and Ken stood eagerly by, hoping for more and bigger fireworks.

But I couldn't stay in the park for ever. And, anyway, said a nasty little voice at the back of my mind, if you don't go home and get filmed, you won't be in the second programme at all, and then you'll get upset like you did last week.

I will *not* get upset, I told myself crossly. So what if I was hardly in the first programme? I didn't care . . . And anyway, what chance did I have of even getting a look-in on Friday's programme? I couldn't compete with Jools and his purple hairdo.

'OI! Come here!'

Startled, I glanced up. The two boys I'd seen before were walking across the grass in my direction, and the puppy was running along in front of them on its wobbly little legs. It was a tiny black and white dog, with floppy ears. It was sweet, but it looked thin, as if it hadn't been fed properly, and I could see that it kept snuffling, as if it had a cold.

One of the boys, who was tall and spotty with a face like a ferret, was trying to catch it.

'You stupid mutt!' he snarled. He made a grab for the puppy, and caught it by its tail. He yanked it viciously, and the puppy yelped in pain. 'Stop running off, or I'll give you what for.'

'What that daft thing needs is a good belting,' said his mate, who had a cigarette hanging out of the corner of his mouth. He aimed a kick at the little dog, who tumbled out of his way, whimpering. 'Then it might do what it's told.'

I gasped. The ferret-faced boy glanced over at me with a nasty grin.

'Yeah, right,' he said loudly. 'Come on, let's find a stick.'

I sat on the edge of the bench, feeling sick and trembling all over. I wasn't stupid or naive. I knew that there were people who were cruel to animals. But to hear it said so suddenly and so casually shook me up inside, especially when I was already feeling so upset.

The puppy toddled over to me, and jumped at my legs. I bent down and stroked its soft ears, and it looked up at me with big velvety eyes. Anger rose up inside me in a huge, overwhelming wave. Suddenly I knew what I had to do. Maybe those boys weren't really going to beat it. Maybe they were just saying that to wind me up because they'd seen I was listening. But I couldn't take that risk.

I bent down. I grabbed the puppy under one arm, and my schoolbag under the other, and then I ran for it. Straight towards the park gates. I'd never, ever stolen anything in my whole life before, and I almost fell over with terror when I heard an angry shout from behind me. But I didn't stop. I raced out into the street, and then, panting with terror, threw a quick glance over my shoulder. The two boys were running after me, their faces contorted with anger.

For a moment my legs just wouldn't move. Then I remembered what they were going to do to the puppy if I didn't get away, and I knew I had to think fast . . .

By the time the boys came out of the gates, I was nowhere to be seen.

'Where the hell's she gone?' I heard one of them wheeze. 'That little –! I'll kill her when I get my hands on her!'

'Your dad's gonna kill *us* if we go back without that dog,' said the other one. 'She couldn't have made it to the end of the road in such a short time. I reckon she must be hiding round here somewhere . . .'

I was. About two feet away from them, actually. The houses that lined both sides of the street were big, posh, detached ones, with large front gardens. I'd dodged into one that had a thick, high hedge separating it from the street, and crouched down behind it, holding the puppy tightly against me. I had my hand over his mouth, so that he didn't whimper and give the game away, but he didn't make a sound. I could feel his heart pounding away in his tiny chest next to my own, and it was almost as if he knew I was trying to save him.

'Yeah, so she's gotta be in one of these gardens then, hasn't she?' I heard the garden gate of the house next door squeak as it was swung open. 'You look in that one, behind the hedge, and I'll go this way.'

I froze with terror. Even through the close-growing leaves, I could see a pair of dirty jeans and even dirtier trainers going past me towards the gate. Any minute now I was going to be discovered –

'What do you two think you're doing?'

I jumped, squeezing the puppy so tightly it squirmed a bit in my arms. Cautiously I peered through the hedge. A big, bald man had come out of one of the gardens across the road, and was glaring at the two boys.

'Keep your hair on, Granddad,' said the ferret-faced boy, and him and his mate both sniggered. 'We're just looking for somebody, OK?'

'No, it's not OK, actually!' the bald man boomed, opening his garden gate. 'We've had a lot of burglaries round here lately, and we don't want the likes of you hanging around. Now go away before I call the police!'

'Yeah? I'm really scared, Baldy!' jeered the ferret-faced boy, but I could see that they both looked just a little bit nervous when the bald man started to walk towards them. He might have been bald, but he was big. Very big.

'OK, OK, we're going!' stuttered Ferret-face, starting to back away down the street. 'No need to get heavy —'

'What about the dog?' his friend hissed at him.

'Oh, stuff the stupid mutt!' the other snapped. 'It ain't worth the effort.'

I heard their footsteps dying away up the street. Then I watched the bald man go back into his garden, and close the gate. I waited a little while longer to make sure it was safe, and then, on trembling legs, I crept out of the garden into the street. I'd never felt so terrified in all my life. And when the puppy put out its little pink tongue and licked my face, I realised for the first time that I was crying. Shaking, I hugged the little dog closer. I wanted my dad.

Even though the two boys were nowhere to be seen by now, I still ran all the way home, the puppy tucked inside my coat and my schoolbag bouncing crazily on my shoulder. I cried all the way, too. I just couldn't seem to stop. When I finally made it, our boring little house with its peeling paint and its scrubby front garden had never looked so good. I was too weak even to get my key out of my pocket, so I just banged on the door and hoped that somebody would come. It seemed like hours before the door finally opened.

'Ally! What's going on? What's happened?' It was Dad. I pitched forward into his arms, still clutching the puppy, and started crying all over again.

'Ally?' Dad drew me gently inside, as I sobbed against the warm, familiar smell of his old jumper. 'What on earth have you been up to, love?'

I lifted my head, and took a breath.

'I was in the park – these two boys – the puppy!' I was crying so hard, I couldn't see straight. 'They hurt it! They kicked it – and – and they were going to beat it with a stick!'

'Ssh.' Dad put his arms round me, and gave me a hug. 'It's all right, love.'

'I – I took the puppy away from them!' I wailed. At that moment the puppy stuck his head out of my coat, and gave a little yelp. 'I stole him!' A sudden, frightening thought struck me. 'Dad, I won't go to prison, will I?'

'Ssh, of course not.' Dad picked the puppy carefully out of my coat, and stroked it. It went wild with joy, licking his hand and wagging its tail. 'Come on, love, everything's going to be all right.'

I looked up at Dad, sniffing, my eyes wide.

'But I *stole* him —'

'Those yobs didn't deserve to have him anyway.' Dad took out his hanky, and gently started to dry my face.

'Can I keep him?' I asked hopefully.

'I think we'd better let the police or the RSPCA know what's happened, and we'll see what they say.'

I gave a sigh of relief, and leaned against Dad. I could always rely on him to get me out of a mess.

'Look at me,' I said with a groan, as I caught sight of myself in the hall mirror. My face was filthy and streaked with tears, and I had bits of leaves and twigs in my hair. 'I look gross –'

And that was when I saw them. Melissa, Nick and Ken. They were standing a little way down the hall, in the living-room doorway, with the camera pointed right in my very muddy and disgusting direction.

A terrible, cold chill swept over me from head to foot.

'Dad,' I said urgently. 'What – I mean – they – they weren't filming us talking just now, were they?'

Dad looked round.

'Good lord, I'd forgotten they were there!' he said, surprised. 'They were just about to interview me in the living room.' He looked at Melissa. 'Were you filming just now?'

'Yes, of course.' Melissa hurried forward, smiling all over her face. 'You were just terrific, Alice. The viewers are going to love hearing how you rescued that poor little puppy.'

I thought I was going to pass out.

'You – you can't show that on TV,' I said, my voice high-pitched with fear. I glanced at myself in the mirror again. I'd cried so much my eyes were swollen, my nose was red and running, and I was muddy all over. I looked truly horrific. 'You *can't*. Please . . .'

'Alice, you were marvellous. Really you were.' Melissa flashed me a warm smile. 'You'll be the star of the show —'

I clutched Dad's hand tighter, and looked up at

him appealingly. Dad nodded comfortingly at me, and then turned to Melissa.

'Alice obviously feels very strongly about this,' he said quietly. 'You don't have to show the film, do you?'

There was a long pause.

'Well, no,' Melissa said reluctantly. Then she shrugged and smiled. 'OK. We definitely won't use it in the programme, if that's what Alice really wants –'

'It is,' I said shakily. 'Thank you.'

'No problem.'

Melissa smiled at me reassuringly, and I managed to smile back, feeling all wobbly with relief. As I did so, I happened to catch Nick's eye as he lowered the camera from his shoulder. And I couldn't help wondering why he was smiling ever so slightly in that not very pleasant way.

Chapter Eight

It was Friday evening, time for the second programme of *Happy Families*.

Happy Families, my foot.

'Oi!' Cindy gave Jools a push that sent him flying as they both raced for the front row armchair. 'I'm sitting there, so you can shove off!'

'You needn't bother,' Jools retorted, giving her a sneaky kick. He'd lied about his hair colour being permanent just to wind Dad up, so Mum had managed to persuade him, with the help of quite a large sum of money, to wash it out. Now he was just faintly plum-coloured. 'You're hardly going to be in it this week, anyway!'

'I don't care!' Cindy snapped back. 'Now that you've washed that pathetic colour out of your hair, nobody's going to be interested in you any more, so there!'

'Cindy, could you ask your mother where she's hidden the remote control?' Dad muttered, plonking himself down furiously on one corner of the sofa.

'Cindy, will you please tell your dad that if he used his eyes for once, he'd see that the remote control is on the table right under his nose!' Mum shot back, plonking herself down in the opposite corner as far away from Dad as possible. Dad and Mum weren't speaking (again) because Dad had found out about Mum bribing Jools, and gone mad. Dad was also in a bad mood because he'd given up smoking (he was about to announce it on air in this week's programme), and Mum was in a bad mood because she was on a diet.

As you can see, being TV stars was beginning to get on everybody's nerves – except mine. In fact, it was quite funny that I was the one who hadn't been that keen to start with, and now I didn't much care about having the camera around (while the others were still slugging it out to see who was going to be a star). I was glad, though, that this week we didn't have Melissa, Nick and Ken crowding into our living room to film us watching the programme. They'd only been interested in filming us watching the first one, so just for tonight we were on our own. They wouldn't be back until early the next morning. It was a weird feeling to be camera-free after the last few weeks. I kept expecting Nick to pop out from behind the sofa at any moment.

I sat on the floor in front of the TV, with Albert the puppy curled up on my lap. He was asleep with both ears flopped over his face, and snoring just a little. Dad had spoken to the police and to the RSPCA, and they'd both said I could keep Albert, but I'd got a bit of a telling-off too, and they'd warned me never to do anything like that again, because I might get hurt. They didn't have to worry. I wasn't planning on doing my animal rescue bit again in the near future – and if I ever did, I'd make sure there wasn't a TV camera around first.

We all sat in silence as the familiar theme music of the programme started. Jools looked excited, Cindy looked sulky and Mum and Dad looked like thunder, like they always did after they'd rowed with each other.

'Tonight,' said the voice-over, 'There's trouble in the Mackenzie household as teenage son Julian decides to assert his individuality . . .'

'Y-e-s!' Jools shouted in triumph as a picture of him coming through the kitchen door with his purple hair flashed up on the screen.

'You're pathetic!' Cindy told him sharply. Mum sniffed, Dad muttered darkly under his breath and I kept quiet.

This week's programme, surprise surprise, was

all about Jools. It showed him going to school with his purple hair, and being marched home by the headmistress. Then Mrs Downey had been interviewed, and said that she couldn't have boys with purple hair lowering the tone of the place, and anyway, purple hair clashed with the red and grey uniform. There was a lot of film of Jools going to town and lurking around in McDonald's while he was suspended, and there were several arguments – a couple between Mum and Dad, and a real stinker of a row between Jools and Dad. Finally, there was a shot of Jools in the bathroom, starting to wash the colour out of his hair. As he turned on the shower spray, he looked at the camera with a cheeky grin and said, 'Next week, I'm going to dye it green.'

Jools hooted with delight as Dad muttered, 'Over my dead body'.

I didn't say anything, but the stupid thing was, I knew that Jools hadn't even *liked* having purple hair. He'd actually told me so yesterday. We'd been sitting in the kitchen on our own, eating beans on toast. Actually, we were eating dry beans on black toast. Jools and I had cooked our tea together, and I'd let the beans boil over while I was helping Jools scrape the black bits off the toast.

'Is that hair colour *really* permanent?' I'd asked

him suddenly, wondering how anybody could go out in public with a head like a flaming beetroot.

Jools had stared at me.

''Course not! You don't think I want to go around looking like this for the rest of my life, do you?'

I shrugged.

'I thought you liked it.'

Jools had hesitated then, obviously trying to decide between keeping up his streetwise image, and telling the truth.

'Not really,' he said at last. 'To be honest, I feel like a right prat. And if you tell Mum and Dad that, I'll kill you.'

'So why did you do it then?' I'd shaken my head wearily. 'No, don't tell me. You wanted to be the star of the show.'

'So what?' Jools had retorted defensively, looking a bit uncomfortable. 'I was fed up with Cindy acting as if she owned the place.'

I hadn't said anything else. I'd just silently hoped that, now both Cindy and Jools had had their own personal taste of stardom, things could get back to normal. Now that the drama of Jools's purple hairdo was over, the programme was showing a very short interview with Dad about why he'd finally decided to give up smoking for good (it was the interview they'd been filming when I'd turned up on the doorstep with Albert). Meanwhile, Cindy was pouting furiously.

'I've hardly been in this stupid programme this week,' she grumbled in a loud voice. 'How much longer is there?'

'Only five minutes or so,' said Mum. And that was when I heard my name.

'So far,' said the voice-over man, 'we haven't seen or heard much of Alice, the youngest of the Mackenzie children. Shyer and quieter than the rest of her family, she has stayed very much in the background –' a picture flashed up of the whole family sitting round the breakfast table, and then the camera changed direction to show me on my own in the corner, writing in my notebook '– but little Alice Mackenzie is not as shy and quiet as you might think . . .'

I sat bolt upright, almost tipping Albert off my lap. The picture on the TV screen had changed, and now there was a shot of Dad walking down the hall to the front door. He opened it, and someone walked in. Someone who was filthy, untidy and crying their eyes out.

It was me.

'Ally!' Dad said on the screen. 'What's going on? What's happened?'

'I was in the park – these two boys – the puppy!' The camera zoomed in on a close-up of my tearstained face, before I buried it in Dad's jumper. 'They hurt it! They kicked it – and – and they were going to beat it with a stick!'

I sat as still on the floor there as if I'd been turned to stone. I couldn't believe what I was seeing. Melissa had *promised* not to show this – and now here it was going out to about twelve million viewers. I was totally shamed. Shamed and humiliated.

The programme showed my conversation with Dad right to the end – at least, until the split-second before I noticed the film crew – and then the credits began to roll. To make things even worse, they left a still of my dirty, tearstained face on the screen, right until the programme ended and the ads started.

There was a shocked silence in the room. Nobody moved. I buried my head in my hands, feeling as if I could never face anybody ever again.

'Dad,' I stammered, tears welling up in my eyes, 'She – she *promised* —'

'I know, Ally.' Dad looked furious, even angrier than he'd been about Jools's purple hairdo, as he got up and came over to me. 'She shouldn't have done it.'

'No, she damn well shouldn't have.' Mum was spitting fire too, her eyes flashing furiously. 'What can we do about it, Dan?'

'I don't know, but I'm going to give that Murray woman a rocket tomorrow morning when she comes back,' Dad said grimly, putting his arm round me.

'Poor old Alice,' Cindy said sympathetically. 'I thought that Melissa was OK, but she's a real cow.'

'Yeah, she is.' Jools reached over and patted Albert's head. 'Don't worry about it, squirt. After all, you're a bit of a heroine.'

'I don't *feel* like a heroine,' I said dolefully, burying my head in Dad's shoulder. 'Everyone at school's going to really take the mickey out of me now.'

'That Melissa Murray's in for a shock tomorrow,' Dad muttered to Mum, who nodded in agreement, her lips folded tightly.

Although I was still upset, I was glad to see that, for almost the first time since the TV cameras had come into our house, the Mackenzies were standing together. All the rows and the backbiting and the jealousy had vanished like magic because they were worried about me. It was a nice, warm feeling.

Enjoy it while it lasts, I told myself grimly, hiding my face in Dad's shoulder. Because tomorrow I'd have to face everyone who'd watched the programme, and seen me covered in mud and leaves and twigs, with a snotty nose and a dirty face, bawling my eyes out . . .

'Dan, I can understand why you're upset —'

'Good. Because we're more than upset, Melissa. We're furious.'

It was the following morning. Dad stood across the kitchen table from Melissa Murray, glaring at her, but she was still managing to look all warm and sympathetic. The rest of us, including me with Albert in my arms, were standing in the kitchen doorway, watching silently. Mum had her arm round me, and even Cindy and Jools looked stern. Dad had insisted that Nick did not film their conversation, and he and Ken stood to one side, drinking coffee and saying nothing.

'Alice particularly asked you not to show that piece of film,' Dad went on furiously. 'You promised her not to show it, and then what do we see last night?'

'Look, Dan, I'm sorry.' I stole a glance at Melissa. I had to admit, she really *did* look sorry. 'I know I said we wouldn't use it, but when

Cameron saw the film back at the studio, he absolutely insisted that Alice's piece go into last night's programme.' She shrugged her shoulders, and looked helplessly at us. 'So what could I do? After all, he *is* my boss, and the producer too. Besides, you *did* sign a contract agreeing that we could show whatever we shot . . .'

I happened to catch Nick's eye then, and, just for a moment, I thought I saw him flash me a sympathetic glance. But it was so quick, I wasn't sure if I'd imagined it.

Dad was still looking grim.

'I know what we signed,' he said tightly. 'I just thought that since we've all got to know each other so well, we could trust you to keep your promise. You've completely upset Alice by showing that piece of film when she didn't want you to —'

'Oh, but there's no need for Alice to feel like that at all!' Melissa swung round and smiled widely at me. Then, leaning over, she grabbed a pile of note papers that lay on the kitchen table. 'Last night we had eighty – yes, eighty – calls from viewers saying how wonderfully brave you'd been, saving the puppy. And look at this!'

Dramatically Melissa started flinging open the Saturday newspapers that also lay on the table.

For the first time, I took a closer look at them. Melissa was pointing at the TV reviews, and suddenly my name was leaping out at me from almost every page. 'Alice the heroine makes *Happy Families* a winner!' read one headline. 'Brave little Alice steals the show!' said another. 'Heroine Alice is the star of the show,' read a third. Some of them even had fuzzy photos of me crying and holding Albert, which they must have taken from the TV screen.

Bewildered, I looked at Melissa.

'I don't understand —'

'Alice, you're a heroine!' Melissa announced with a big smile. 'The viewers love you, and so do the papers!'

I gaped at her.

'They do?'

'See? Things haven't turned out so badly, have they?' Melissa wagged her finger at me teasingly. 'Right, so what we want to do this morning is to concentrate on you, Alice. I thought it would be really excellent if we could shoot an interview with you, ask you about your rescue of the puppy in more detail. All right?'

I stared at her. I couldn't get my head round what was happening. Last week I'd been on screen for about half a minute, and now here I was being called the star of the show. Did I *want* to be the star of the show? How did I really feel about it?

I thought hard for a few seconds. I felt scared, and still a bit unsure of myself. But underneath it all, yes, I definitely felt excited.

'All right,' I said to Melissa in a wobbly voice.

'Are you sure, Ally?' Dad frowned. 'We don't want you being forced into anything you don't want to do.' He glared at Melissa. 'Again.'

I shook my head.

'It's fine, Dad.' And suddenly I realised that I was looking forward to being interviewed.

'OK, then, Nick, let's set up in the living room, and we'll interview her there.' Melissa turned away and started giving instructions to Nick and Ken. Meanwhile, Jools and Cindy were laughing.

'Well done, squirt!' Cindy said generously. 'Looks like you're the new star of the show!'

Jools slapped me on the back.

'Yeah, but don't dye your hair purple, OK?' he said solemnly, and we all burst out laughing.

After breakfast, Melissa ushered me into the living room, along with Albert, sat me down on the sofa and told me the kind of questions she was going to ask me. I was pretty nervous because this was the very first time I'd been filmed on my own, and having Nick's camera pointing at me, and just me, was a bit frightening. My knees were wobbling and my throat felt a bit dry, but Melissa told me not to worry. If I made a mistake, or seized up, they would simply film it again.

'OK, Nick.' Melissa took up her position by the cameraman's side. 'Let's go.'

I stroked Albert nervously and tried to look heroine-like as Melissa smiled at me.

'So, Alice, tell us exactly what happened when you rescued Albert the puppy here.'

I cleared my throat.

'Well, I was on my way home from school —' my voice turned into a squeak from nerves, and I stopped, feeling embarrassed.

'Don't worry.' Melissa jumped in immediately. 'We'll start again.'

In the end it took about eight takes to get the interview right. Melissa wanted to do take after take because she kept thinking of things I could say, and suggesting them to me. She wanted to 'really tug the viewers' heartstrings', she said. And she seemed pretty pleased with the result too.

'Well done, Alice!' She beamed at me, and I glowed with pleasure. 'You were brilliant!'

'Thanks,' I muttered, feeling a bit embarrassed. I thought that maybe I'd gone a bit over the top, going on and on about how those two boys had been mistreating Albert, but that had been what Melissa wanted.

'You really were brave, you know,' Melissa went on warmly. 'I expect you've written all about rescuing Albert in your diary, haven't you?'

'My diary?' I stared at her.

Melissa smiled at me.

'That book you're always writing in.'

'Oh, that's not a diary exactly. It's my Top Secret Notebook,' I said, and then I blushed. I never talked to *anyone* about what was in my notebook, except Dad sometimes.

'Top Secret Notebook?' Melissa repeated, looking interested. 'What's in it?'

I shuffled my feet, and looked down at the floor.

'Oh, stories, poems, bits and pieces . . .' I said reluctantly. Melissa's face lit up as if somebody had told her she'd won the lottery.

'So you're a writer, are you? Maybe we could film you reading some of your work some time. I'm sure the viewers would love to see that.'

A thrill of excitement and panic ran through me.

'I – don't know,' I said slowly. 'I'm not sure . . .'

'Well, have a think about it, and let me know. Oh, and while I remember –' Melissa swept on regardless '– would you possibly reconsider your decision not to allow us to film you at school? I really think the viewers would love to see more of you, and filming you at school would be a great angle.'

I looked at Melissa. Well, what could I say?

'Um – OK then . . .'

'Wonderful!' Melissa looked like I'd made her day. 'I'll give your head teacher a ring straight-away,' and she went off into a corner with her mobile phone.

Still stunned by my speedy transformation from boring schoolgirl to child superstar, I put Albert on the floor and started hunting for his lead. I'd promised to take him round to Francine's this morning, and we were going to go to the park. I started giggling to myself as I thought of what Francine would say when she found out I was now the star of the show. She was going to be dead jealous!

'I can't get through at the moment.' Clicking her tongue with annoyance, Melissa shoved her mobile phone back into her handbag. 'I'll try again later. Where are you going now, Alice?'

I found Albert's lead under the sofa, and clipped it onto his collar.

'I said I'd go round to Francine's —'

'OK,' Melissa said briskly. 'Nick, can you get packed up quickly, and Ken, we might need some extra equipment at Francine's house, so can you sort that out.'

I stared at her.

'You mean – you're coming with me?'

'Of course.' Melissa looked at me as if I was crazy. 'Alice, you've got to get it into your head – *you're* the Mackenzie the viewers want to see at the moment!'

'Fine.' Still feeling dazed, I managed a weak smile. 'Hold on, I won't be a minute . . .'

I went out of the room, and ran up the stairs, two at a time, Albert snapping at my heels. My heart pounding with excitement, I flung open the bedroom door. Cindy was inside, doing her nails.

'Oh, hi,' she said, glancing up. 'Finished your interview?'

'Yep, and now they're going to film me going to Francine's!' I gabbled breathlessly, pulling open my wardrobe. 'What do you think I should wear?'

Cindy thought for a moment.

'How about that new skirt, and your blue top?' she suggested.

'OK.' I threw off my old sweatshirt and jeans, and started struggling into my new clothes. I could hardly believe this was happening to me.

Me, Alice Mackenzie! Quiet, shy, boring, little Alice Mackenzie. And what was even more unbelievable – I was enjoying it too. Then a sudden thought struck me.

'Cindy?' I said hesitantly, turning to look at her. 'You don't mind them filming me, do you?'

Cindy grinned at me.

'No, of course not. Actually –' she looked a bit embarrassed '– I think me and Jools went way over the top the last few weeks. You enjoy it while it lasts.'

'Thanks.' I smiled back at her, and ran downstairs.

The walk to Francine's house was unbelievable. Almost as soon as I set foot out of the house, our neighbours from next door and across the road came out to talk about the programme, and tell me how brave I'd been. Then when I reached the main road, people I didn't even know kept on coming up to me, and congratulating me, and wanting to stroke Albert. Nick filmed it all, while Melissa stood and watched with a pleased smile on her face. I could guess what she was thinking – this is going to make great television.

'You're a heroine, my dear,' said one little old lady, who came up to me and patted me on the back. 'A real heroine.'

Was I a heroine? I asked myself as we finally reached Francine's house. I was still the same old Alice Mackenzie I'd always been. But perhaps not. Overnight I seemed to have turned into a different person. A much more glamorous, interesting person. It was scary in a way, but incredibly exciting.

I rang Francine's doorbell. Francine's mum pulled back the curtain, saw us and let out a screech. Not surprising really, as she was in her dressing-gown and curlers. There was the sound of footsteps thundering all over the house, and a voice yelling 'For heaven's sake, clear up that mess in the living room!', and finally Francine opened the door, her face red with excitement.

'Hi!' she squeaked, staring at the camera as if she was mesmerised. 'Are they really filming?'

''Fraid so,' I said apologetically. 'Is it all right if we come in?'

'Sure,' Francine stammered, goggling.

'OK, Nick, cut.' Melissa ordered. 'We'll set up inside, and film the two girls chatting.' She swept into the house as if she owned it, and went straight up to Francine's mum who was hiding behind the living-room door, trying to take her curlers out at top speed. 'Hello, Mrs West, I'm Melissa Murray from Harlequin TV . . .'

'Alice, what's going on?' Francine hissed at me, her eyes like saucers.

'Did you see the programme last night?' I asked her, standing aside to let Nick and Ken follow Melissa into the house.

'Yeah, 'course I did!' Francine said eagerly. 'Did you go mad when they showed that film of you and Albert?'

'Well, I wasn't very pleased at first,' I admitted honestly. 'But it's kind of made me into a bit of a heroine. I'm all over today's papers!'

'Wow!' Francine gasped. 'So now you're the star of the show?'

'It looks like it,' I said hesitantly. 'It all feels a bit weird, really . . .' I stood in front of Francine on the doorstep, and put my hands on my hips. 'Do I look any different to you this morning?'

Francine looked me carefully up and down.

'Nope,' she said at last. 'You look exactly the same as you did yesterday.'

'That's what I mean ,' I sighed. 'I'm not *really* any different, am I?'

Francine rolled her eyes.

'Oh, stop moaning!' she said briskly. 'You're a lucky pig, Alice Mackenzie, and I wish it was *me* who was the star of a TV programme, so there!'

‘So what do you think I should do then?’ I asked her.

‘Enjoy it, that’s what!’ Francine said firmly.

‘Mm.’ I hesitated. ‘You know, France, I was thinking . . .’

‘Did it hurt?’

‘Ha ha. Look, I was thinking, when all those people were coming up to me this morning . . .’ I hesitated, trying to find the words to explain. ‘I suddenly thought, that if that programme last night stopped just one person from being cruel to animals, then I did some good, didn’t I?’

Francine put her hands on my shoulders, and stood on tiptoe.

‘What’re you doing?’ I asked, bewildered.

‘Looking for your halo,’ Francine giggled. ‘Oh, yeah, there it is, all gold and sparkly.’

‘Shut up!’ I gave her a friendly push. ‘I’m not in this just to be a star, like Jools and Cindy were. I want to do some *good*. You see what I mean, don’t you?’

‘’Course I do.’ Francine nodded at me. ‘St Alice, patron saint of animals *and* glamorous TV star!’

We both started giggling, and then Melissa’s voice floated out along the hallway.

‘Alice, we’re ready for you and Francine now, please.’

'Gosh, what it is to be a star!' Francine said soulfully, clasping her hands dramatically as we went indoors.

We burst out giggling all over again, but inside I was thinking hard. I'd meant what I'd said to Francine. Because people wanted to watch me on TV and listen to what I had to say, suddenly I had some *power*. And maybe I could use that power to do some good for things I really cared about. Like stopping people from being cruel to animals, for a start.

Yep, I thought solemnly, as I switched on a smile for Nick's camera, being a TV star was turning out to be a big responsibility . . .

Chapter Nine

' – and so Jemima the elephant had to stay in the zoo for the rest of her life. But she never forgot the big, open spaces in Africa where she was born. And every night she would lie sleeping in the small, cramped elephant house at the zoo, and dream that she was at home, under the African moon.'

Embarassed, I closed my Top Secret Notebook, and cleared my throat.

'Well done, Alice!' Melissa beamed at me from behind the camera on Nick's shoulder. 'That was perfect!'

It was early in the morning, just before I was due to set off for school, and after a lot of persuasion from Melissa I'd finally agreed to be filmed reading one of the stories I'd written in my Top Secret Notebook. It was about an elephant who lived in a zoo, but who kept trying to escape, and get back to its home in Africa. I'd written it after watching a really horrible TV programme about zoos, and how some of them didn't look after their animals properly. I hadn't really want to read *anything* out at all, but Melissa had gone on and on about how much she wanted me to do it. And I'd told myself that if it made people think about being kinder to animals, then it'd be worth it. After all, I couldn't carry on being all shy and retiring now that I was a TV star, could I?

'OK, Nick, let's get packed up and ready to go,' Melissa was saying briskly. Today was the day that she and the crew were coming to school with me for the first time, and I was actually looking forward to being filmed in class, now that I was getting to be an old hand in front of the cameras.

Just then the doorbell rang.

'That'll be Francine,' I said breathlessly. When I'd told France that the cameras would be coming to school with us on Monday, she'd almost passed out with excitement. Oh, well, I thought with a knowing smile, she'll soon get used to it.

I ran to the front door. It *was* Francine standing outside, but I almost didn't recognise her. She had her dark, frizzy hair which was she always moaning about tied up in a high ponytail on top of her head with a red ribbon, and she had tiny gold hoops in her ears. Her school uniform was spotless, and when I looked a bit closer, I could see she was wearing lip gloss and mascara. She looked – good . . .

I stared at her, feeling a sudden and very unpleasant wave of jealousy sweep over me.

'What've you gone and done to yourself?' I asked shortly.

Francine giggled.

'Well, if we're going to be filmed today, I want to look my best, don't I?'

I gave her a not-too-friendly stare.

'Does your mum know?'

'Nope. The baby threw his cereal at the dog this morning, so while Mum was clearing that up, I nicked some of her make-up and sneaked out before she saw me.' Francine preened herself on the doorstep. 'What do you think?'

'It's OK,' I muttered sourly. 'But Munro's going to shred you when she sees it.'

'I'll risk it,' Francine said confidently. Then a big smile split her face as she saw Melissa, Ken and Nick coming up the hall towards us. 'Are we going now?'

'Oh, hello, Francine.' Melissa gave her a little wave over my head. 'You look nice today.'

I frowned as Francine beamed back at her. What was going on? *I* was supposed to be the star of the show, wasn't I?

'We'll take you down to school in the van, and film you going in through the school gates, to begin with,' Melissa said briskly. 'I've cleared everything with your headmaster.'

'Oh, this is going to be so exciting!' Francine chirped happily. She slipped her arm though mine as we all went down the path, and I immediately felt ashamed of my jealousy a moment before. What was the matter with me? It wasn't as if I was obsessed with the idea of being a star like Jools and Cindy, was it?

When we arrived at our school, we had a bit of a shock. Although we were early, it looked like everybody else had arrived before us. There were teachers hanging out of every window, and the playground was already full of kids. As soon as they spotted the van, there was a shout of delight, and a stampede towards the gates. Francine and I gasped as a crowd of about three hundred kids charged straight towards us, yelling and waving. Suddenly I knew how it must've felt to be Madonna. Without any bodyguards.

But Melissa wasn't having any of it. With a steely glint in her eye, she leapt out of the van and put her hands on her hips.

'HOLD IT RIGHT THERE!' she yelled.

The mob skidded to a collective halt under Melissa's eagle eye, but they still carried on yelling and screaming. Melissa didn't flinch. She simply waited until the last shout had died away, and then she spoke.

'Right! As you obviously know, we're going to be filming Alice Mackenzie here today' – embarrassed, I slid down in the van until only the top of my head could be seen through the windscreen '– and we'll probably be filming some of you as well, *but only* if you behave yourselves, and do as you're told. Is that clear?'

The crowd nodded sheepishly.

'Wow!' said Francine admiringly. 'Melissa could thrash Munro in a shouting-contest any day. She's got attitude!'

'Ah, Miss Murray . . .' As Francine and I were climbing out of the van, the headmaster suddenly appeared out of the school door, and rushed over to us. 'Sorry, I didn't see you arrive. I was on the phone —'

'Melissa Murray. Nice to meet you.' In the blink of an eye, Melissa changed from steely-eyed super-heroine into efficient but charming TV director. Francine and I glanced at each other and giggled. 'Now, d'you think you could stand guard and keep all these kids away from the gates while we're filming Alice and Francine?'

Robbo blinked. I don't think he'd done playground duty since about 1970. Now that he was a head teacher, herding groups of kids around was a bit below his dignity.

'Er – right.' He shot one of his glares at the kids crowding round, and they started to drift away reluctantly. 'Now, I expect you'd like to film me coming over and saying good morning to Alice and Francine as they come through the gates?'

Francine and I looked at each other again, and had to bite our lips to stop ourselves laughing.

'Well, not unless you make a habit of coming out to say hello to every pupil when they arrive in the morning?' Melissa said coolly.

Robbo shuffled his feet a bit, and looked like a naughty kid.

'Um – well - no, I don't . . .'

'Well, we *do* want to keep things as normal as possible, really.' Melissa gave him a melting smile. 'It *would* be very helpful if you could keep the children under control just for the moment. And we'll definitely be filming an interview with you later on.'

'Really?' Robbo looked as if someone had just given him a million pounds. 'Well, that's fine. Good. Wonderful. Michael Parker! If you don't get away from that camera, I shall personally come over there and give you five detentions . . .'

I don't know why I'd refused to be filmed at school before, because it was just the *best* fun ever.

Nick, Melissa and Ken followed me all over the place, filming my every move. They filmed me hanging up my coat in the cloakroom, going into class, going into assembly – the lot. Miss Munro was so thrilled about being filmed, especially when Melissa said they wanted to interview her too, that she gave me all the best jobs in class. In fact, she was so excited, she didn't even notice Francine's lipgloss. Francine said if she'd have known she could have got away with it, she'd have borrowed her mum's diamanté earrings too. So, after being the wicked witch who wouldn't let everybody get a taste of TV stardom, I was now everybody's blue-eyed girl. I was having a ball.

In fact, the only bad thing about the whole day was that I had a row with Francine. Well, not exactly a row. More a sort of minor disagreement. Francine getting her knickers in a twist over nothing at all, really . . .

It started that afternoon when Nick, Ken and Melissa were filming us in class. Francine and I were working on our project, which was about endangered species. It had been Francine's idea to do it, and I was glad we'd chosen it, because it was something I felt strongly about. Melissa started looking through our folder at the work we'd done so far, and asking me all about it.

'Some of these drawings are really excellent.' Melissa pointed at a picture of a baby elephant standing next to its mother, and Nick's camera zoomed in for a close-up. 'So what made you choose the topic of endangered species for your project, Alice?'

'I chose to do it because I'm worried about the way some animals are disappearing from our world,' I told her sadly. 'People take animals like tigers and pandas for granted, but there really aren't many of them left.'

'You care a lot about animals and the environment, don't you, Alice?' Melissa said.

I looked solemnly into Nick's camera.

'Of course I do. Everybody should, not just kids, but grown-ups too. That's why I wanted to do this project, to make people realise that if these animals die out, it's our fault.'

'OK, Nick, cut.' Melissa flashed me a smile. 'Well done, Alice. That should make a few of our viewers think.'

I smiled back, feeling quite pleased with myself. I was beginning to realise exactly how much power I suddenly had because I was on TV. People would listen to what I had to say, and maybe they'd even do something about it – join a campaign group to save the rain forests or whatever. And it would all be down to me.

'I never realised before just how much TV can change things,' I said thoughtfully. 'Do you think people who watch the programme will *really* take any notice of me?'

'Of course!' Melissa said sincerely. Then she gave me a serious look. 'Never underestimate the power of TV, Alice. And that reminds me, there's something very important I want to discuss with you . . .'

The bell for playtime rang out just then.

'Are you going to come out into the playground with me?' I asked Melissa curiously, wondering what she wanted to talk to me about.

She shook her head.

'Not just yet. We've arranged to film an interview with your headmaster now. We'll see you later, though.'

'Well, that went off pretty well, didn't it?' I said to Francine as we went out into the playground. I tried not to sound too pleased with myself. Although I'd begun what looked like being a one-girl campaign to change the world, I still had a long way to go.

Francine didn't say anything. I glanced over at her, and was surprised to see that she looked upset, for some reason.

'Hey, what's up with you?' I asked with a frown.

Francine glared at me.

'Well, you should know!' she burst out furiously.

'What?' I said in an injured tone. 'I haven't done anything!'

'Oh, haven't you?' Francine snapped, 'Maybe I'm going wacko or something, but I thought it was *my* idea to do our project about endangered species?'

I looked at her, bewildered.

'So?'

'So, when Melissa was interviewing you, you made out that it was *your* idea to do the project – *and* you didn't even tell her that those drawings were MINE!'

I stared at her.

'Is that all?'

'WHAT DO YOU MEAN – IS THAT ALL!' Francine hollered at me.

'What I mean is, you're losing your cool over nothing at all!' I snapped back. 'Look, it doesn't matter who thought of the project! It's more important that people listen to what I've got to say. And anyway, *I'm* the star of the show, not you – even if you *are* wearing your mum's make-up!'

The moment the words were out of my mouth, I wished I hadn't said them. They sounded mean and jealous and nasty. I felt even worse when I saw that Francine was trembling on the verge of tears, and that her mascara was ever so slowly beginning to smudge.

'Francine —' I said quickly.

'Oh, get lost!' she snapped at me, and she turned and walked away.

See what I mean?

OK, I thought, trying to be fair as I sat by myself in the playground, maybe Francine had a point. Maybe it *had* been a bit much of me to claim that the project was my idea, but over the last few weeks I'd learned enough about the way TV worked to know that sometimes the truth had to be stretched to make a point. Melissa quite often asked us to do things again if she'd thought of something to make the scene look even better; sometimes she'd even suggest things we could say, like she'd done when I'd been interviewed about Albert. The way I saw it, the people who watched *Happy Families* would take more notice of *me* telling them about endangered species than they would of Francine, because I was the one they wanted to see. I just wished I could have explained that to Francine, without making her so mad. We hadn't had a row like that for years. Not since I borrowed her new bike without asking, and crashed it into a milk float.

Anyway, Francine didn't speak to me for the rest of the afternoon. I couldn't try and make up with her either, because Melissa, Nick and Ken were filming me again, and I didn't really want to tell them what had happened. Of course, Melissa noticed that Francine and I weren't speaking, and asked me what was going on, but I managed to change the subject.

I didn't get a chance to speak to Francine again because, as soon as school finished, Melissa, Ken and Nick took me straight over to the local park, the same park where I'd rescued Albert. Melissa wanted me to point out to the viewers the exact spot where I'd taken him from the two boys. There was also a big pond in the middle of the park that was polluted and full of people's rubbish, and Melissa thought it would be a good subject for me to talk about for the next week's programme.

When we finally arrived home from the park, I was really tired. Being a TV star and having to be on my best behaviour all day was exhausting – and anyway, the argument I'd had with Francine had been on my mind all the time we were filming by the pond, so it had taken me an hour (and about ten million takes) to get it right. So I was really glad to be home at last. But when I staggered into the living room, ready to be the couch potato champion of all time, I walked head-on into a row between Cindy and Mum.

'Oh, Mum, give it a rest!' Cindy was shouting crossly. 'I'll tidy the bedroom when I get back. I told you, I'm meeting Jackie in five minutes!'

'You said that yesterday, and the day before!' Mum snapped. 'Your bedroom looks like a bomb's hit it, and you're not going anywhere until you've cleared it up! There were eight dirty coffee mugs on your bedside table at the last count!'

'They're not mine – they're Alice's!' Cindy retorted.

'I don't even drink coffee!' I said indignantly. I was a bit annoyed to see that, at a nod from Melissa, Nick had swung the camera away from me, and zoomed in on Cindy and Mum's angry faces.

'Oh, it's not fair!' Cindy announced, tossing back her gleaming blonde hair so that Nick could get a better shot of her face. 'I tidied *my* stuff up this morning. That mess is all Alice's rubbish —'

'It is not!' I said indignantly. Just then, out of the corner of my eye, I caught Melissa staring hard at me. She was out of shot, as she always was, but she was nodding at me, and pointing upstairs. Suddenly I understood what she wanted me to do.

'Anyway,' Cindy was saying loudly, 'it's not *that* bad —'

'Oh, isn't it?' I interrupted her. Then I swung round, ran across the living room and beckoned to the film crew. 'Come on!'

Nick, Ken and Melissa raced out of the room after me, and Melissa flashed me an approving grin as we all ran upstairs.

'Oi!' I could hear Cindy shouting behind us. 'What d'you think you're doing?'

I didn't stop until I reached our bedroom door. Then I waited for Nick and Ken to get into position before I threw it open.

'Take a look for yourselves!' I announced.

The camera panned around our bedroom. My side was neat and tidy like it usually was. Cindy's was a mess. In fact, it was even worse than usual. Her bed wasn't made, and you couldn't see the carpet on her side of the room for the weight of clothes, books, CDs, magazines and make-up lying on it.

There was the sound of a mad elephant rampaging up the stairs, and then Cindy appeared, red in the face, with Mum close behind her.

'So you've tidied it up, have you? Good,' said Mum, her voice dripping with sarcasm. 'I dread to think what it looked like *before*.'

'All right, all right, I'll do it now!' Cindy marched past us all with her nose in the air, and gave me a stare of pure poison. 'Thanks a lot, brat! I'll embarrass *you* on nation-wide TV sometime!'

As Cindy slammed the bedroom door in all our faces, I felt a bit uncomfortable. I shouldn't really have done that, I thought unhappily. But our bedroom *was* a mess. I was always going on at Cindy to clear it up. And besides, it had been Melissa's idea to come upstairs and film it, not mine . . .

Mum had gone downstairs to make some coffee, and Nick and Ken had gone with her. I stayed on the landing, wondering whether I ought to go into our bedroom, and say sorry to Cindy. I didn't fancy the idea much. From the bangs and thumps I could hear from behind the closed door, she was throwing everything around the room in a temper.

I thought Melissa had gone down with the others, until I heard her voice behind me.

'What's the matter, Alice? Are you OK? You look a bit upset.'

I shuffled my feet uneasily.

'I feel a bit mean about dropping Cindy in it like that,' I admitted gloomily. I wondered if there was any point in asking Melissa not to use the film in this Friday's programme, and decided that there wasn't. Not after all the drama with Albert. 'Maybe I shouldn't have done it . . .'

'Look, Alice, this is real life we're filming here, and nobody's perfect.' Melissa put her hand on my shoulder sympathetically. 'We want to see your family as they *really* are. And anyway –' she looked solemnly at me '– sometimes it takes a short, sharp shock to make people wake up to themselves. If this makes Cindy tidy her side of your bedroom up from now on, it'll have been worth it, won't it?'

I thought for a moment or two.

'Yes,' I said at last, feeling better.

Melissa smiled at me.

'Remember what I said to you this afternoon? That I wanted to talk something over with you?'

I nodded. After all the rows with Francine and Cindy, I'd forgotten about that.

'Well . . .' Melissa went on slowly, 'the programme's going pretty well at the moment, but I still feel that there's more we could be doing.'

'What do you mean?'

'Well, I still don't feel that we've seen the *real*

Mackenzies yet,' Melissa said softly. 'I mean, your dad says he's given up smoking, but has he really? I noticed a packet of cigarettes in his jacket pocket the other day.'

'Dad's tried to give up smoking about a million times,' I said, shaking my head. 'And he hasn't managed it yet.'

'Maybe we could do something about that,' Melissa suggested quietly.

I looked at her curiously.

'How?'

Melissa grinned at me.

'Is there somewhere quiet we can go and talk?'

Chapter Ten

'Nearly time for *Happy Families* to start,' I announced, plumping myself down in the most comfy armchair, the one closest to the TV set. 'I wonder what this week's programme'll be like?'

'They'd better not show that bit about our bedroom,' Cindy muttered under her breath, throwing me a haughty stare. She still hadn't *quite* forgiven me for that, but it had worked. She'd kept our bedroom loads tidier this week, so it had been worth it in the end.

'Oh, shut up, Cindy,' Jools said lazily from the other end of the sofa. 'Just 'cos Alice got one over on you, and now she's the star of the show.'

'I think it's brilliant the way Alice has come out of her shell over the last few weeks,' Mum said warmly, dropping a kiss on top of my head. 'Don't you, Dan?'

'Yep, she's turning out to be a proper little Mackenzie show-off!' Dad said, giving me a teasing grin.

'Sssh! It's starting!' I hissed, as the theme music began.

'This week on *Happy Families*,' said the voice-over, 'the Mackenzies as you've never seen them before . . .'

'What's that supposed to mean?' Mum asked, looking puzzled.

I smiled to myself. I was the *only* person who knew what was going to happen in the programme tonight. Melissa and I had worked it all out between us, and we'd managed to film masses of stuff secretly, without Mum, Dad, Cindy and Jools realising what was going on. It was going to be a big surprise when they found out . . .

The first part of the programme was me reading out my story. I found it incredibly embarrassing, and pulled a cushion over my head so I didn't have to listen to it, but my family were impressed.

'Alice, that was brilliant!' Cindy said, her eyes round. 'I didn't know you wrote all that stuff!'

'Oh, I think it's wonderful.' Mum wiped a couple of tears from her eyes. 'My little Alice a TV star!'

'You'll have the kids at school asking for your autograph on Monday!' Jools said with a grin.

The programme went on to show some of the

film they'd shot of me at school, but not very much. Miss Munro's interview wasn't shown at all, and even Robbo only got about fifteen seconds on air, saying what a nice well-behaved girl I was, and how I always got good marks in English.

Then, suddenly, Robbo's bald head vanished from the screen, and the picture changed. Dad was sitting in the kitchen, and Mum walked in, carrying a load of shopping bags.

'Oh, I know what this bit is,' said Mum from the corner of the sofa where she was sitting. 'This is when I start going on about my diet.'

Dad frowned.

'What're they showing this for? It's not exactly very interesting.'

I bit my lip to hold back my giggles. Not very interesting? Wait till they saw what came next!

On the telly, Mum put her bags down on the kitchen table, and began telling Dad how much weight she was losing on her diet.

MUM: Well, I think I've lost about five pounds now, Dan. Isn't that great?

DAD (grumpily): Looks like you've lost a lot more than five pounds! How much have you spent?

MUM: Oh, don't be such an old misery! I haven't spent very much. I just bought a dress. It was a bargain, only £39.99 (Mum pulls dress out of

carrier bag, and shows it to the camera).
DAD: £39.99! And that'll never fit you – it's too small!
MUM: I know it won't fit me now, but it'll fit me when I've lost some more weight . . .

Dad groaned as we all watched him pulling a face on the screen at the camera.

'Your mother thinks I'm made of money!'

'Sssh!' I hissed urgently. 'Don't miss this bit!'

'Like all families, the Mackenzies have their little secrets,' said the voice-over man, and suddenly there was my face filling the screen again. 'So maybe Alice can tell us a little bit more about them . . .'

'LITTLE SECRETS?' repeated Mum, Dad, Cindy and Jools together, all looking puzzled. 'What's going on?'

'Wait and see!' I said under my breath.

'Look, what's that Alice is holding?' Jools asked curiously.

We all looked at the TV. On the screen, I was smiling and holding up a piece of paper. The camera zoomed in for a close-up. It was a shop receipt for a dress costing £59.99.

'What on earth —?' said Dad, bewildered.

'EEK!' Mum squealed in dismay. 'That's the receipt for the dress I bought!'

'What?' Dad roared. 'You told me it was only £39.99!'

Cindy and Jools collapsed in hysterical giggles, and I couldn't help laughing too. I'd mentioned to Melissa that Mum never told Dad what she paid for *anything* – it was a family joke. So Melissa had suggested that I get hold of the dress receipt, and they would film it. She'd said it would be really funny, as well as showing 'the real side of family life'. And there was more to come . . .

'Don't miss this bit!' I yelled over the laughter.

'As we all know, Barbara Mackenzie is on a diet,' said the voice-over man. 'Let's find out how it's going . . .'

I was back on-screen again. Nick had filmed me creeping down the hall towards the kitchen. Silently I'd pushed the door open just a little bit, Nick had filmed secretly through the gap – and there was Mum standing by the kitchen sink with the biscuit tin, munching a custard cream, followed by four chocolate digestives.

'Oh NO!' Cindy squealed, tears of laughter pouring down her face. 'You've really been shamed now, Mum!'

'Brilliant!' Jools was rolling on the floor, holding his sides. 'Caught on film scoffing biscuits, when you're supposed to be on a diet!'

I was laughing too. Until I caught a glimpse of Mum's face.

'Alice, how *could* you?' she said in a stifled voice.

I stared at Mum, feeling suddenly guilty. I hadn't expected her to look so hurt. Oh, I'd thought she might be a *bit* mad to begin with, but I'd sort of thought she'd see the funny side. Maybe I shouldn't have done it after all . . . As I remembered what was still to come in the programme, I felt a cold shiver run down my spine. But Melissa had said it would be OK, hadn't she? She'd even said it would be great television . . .

'But Barbara isn't the only member of the family who has a little secret,' the voice-over went on. A picture flashed up on screen of Dad, with a smugly virtuous smile on his face, throwing his cigarettes in the dustbin. 'Remember last week's programme, when Dan swore he was giving up smoking for good?'

Dad sat up in his chair, and I slid down in mine, trying to make myself as small as possible.

I was back on screen again. Melissa and I had spent a whole afternoon when everyone else was out, searching all over the house for Dad's secret supplies of ciggies. Then Nick had filmed me running into every room, and pointing out where they all were. On the TV now, I was in the bathroom, opening the cupboard. There, hidden under a pile of razors, was a packet of cigarettes. There was also a packet hidden under the sofa, in a pot plant, behind the fridge, and even one in Albert's basket, under his cushion.

Cindy and Jools were roaring with laughter, Dad looked stunned and Mum looked furious.

'So you've given up smoking, have you, Daniel?' she enquired in an icy voice, and I couldn't help giggling. Dad didn't say anything. He just stared at me without saying a word, and I stopped laughing, and began feeling uncomfortable instead. Still, it wasn't my fault if everyone went around telling fibs, was it? And I was only doing what Melissa had asked me to do – show what the Mackenzies were *really* like . . .

'This is just brilliant!' Cindy gurgled, hiccuping with laughter. 'Serves you both right!'

'Hey, wait a minute!' Jools said suddenly. He was staring at the TV. 'That's my bedroom!'

'As you may remember,' the voice-over went on, 'teenager Jools can be a bit of a rebel. But he has his soft side too . . .'

'What?' Jools sat bolt upright. 'What does he mean – a soft side?'

I bit my lip. Melissa had asked me if Jools had

any 'little secrets', and I'd told her I thought he kept his old teddy bear Boris under his bed. The film crew and I had gone into Jools's room one afternoon when he'd gone to see one of his mates, to check it out. Now, on the TV screen, a hand (mine) was slowly pulling back the duvet – and there, sitting under the bed, wrapped lovingly in a blanket, was a moth-eaten old teddy with one ear hanging off.

'NO!' Jools yelped as if he was in pain, and clutched at his forehead, his eyes wild. 'Who told that cow Melissa about that?' His eyes swivelled accusingly round, and met mine.

'You little —!' Jools lunged across the room towards me, and had to be forcibly restrained by Dad. 'I can never face my mates again!'

I stared at him, my lips trembling.

'Sorry,' I said in a small voice. I was beginning to realise that maybe I'd got a bit carried away. But when I'd suggested all this stuff to Melissa, she'd said it was just the kind of thing she was looking for. And I hadn't thought that everyone would be *quite* so upset. After all, it was just a bit of fun . . .

Cindy was glaring at me menacingly.

'I hope there's nothing in this programme about *me*, Alice Mackenzie!' she snapped, 'or I'll —'

'We all know just how glamorous the

Mackenzies' elder daughter Cindy is,' said the voice-over man right at that moment, as my heart sank down into my shoes. 'And she obviously gets plenty of beauty sleep . . .'

On the screen, a hand (mine) swung open our bedroom door. As Nick's camera moved inside, a loud snore resounded across the room. We'd sneaked upstairs to film Cindy one morning when she was having a lie-in, and there she was, flat on her back, snoring like a pig, with cream all over her face, and rollers in her hair. She'd been so fast asleep, she hadn't even woken up when Melissa and I had started giggling.

'Eeek!' Cindy screeched, leaping to her feet. 'You – you —!' For once words failed her, and she could only glare at me.

There was uproar in the whole room now. Everyone was shouting at me and at each other so loudly, we couldn't even hear the theme music as the programme finished. I didn't say anything. I just slumped down in my chair, and hoped a big hole would open and swallow me right up. I was beginning to wish I'd never heard of Melissa Murray and *Happy Families*.

'Right, that's ENOUGH!' Dad roared over the noise. He looked at me, and I felt a tremor of alarm run through me. I hadn't seen Dad give me a look like that before. Ever. 'I think Alice has got some explaining to do.'

Everyone turned and I wilted under the glare of four pairs of furious eyes.

'What's the matter?' I mumbled, looking down at my feet. 'Melissa said it would only be a bit of fun —'

'Ah, Melissa. I might've guessed,' Dad said grimly. 'I'm beginning to wonder if we haven't all been wrong about her.'

'Melissa's OK,' I muttered defensively. 'She said she just wanted to show the real side of family life, that's all.'

'Oh yeah?' Jools shouted at me. 'Well, how come *you're* the only one of us who wasn't made to look a complete prat tonight?'

'What about last week then?' I reminded him. 'It was *me* who was made to look an idiot with all that fuss over Albert.'

'But that wasn't down to us, though, was it?' Dad said quietly, looking me straight between the eyes. 'As I remember, we were all on your side against Melissa.'

I suddenly felt horribly ashamed of myself. Dad was right. Everybody had stood by me last week when I'd been so upset about the Albert drama being shown on air. And what had I done? Turned round and slapped them in the face, that's what.

'Sorry,' I muttered, biting my lip.

Cindy and Jools didn't answer. They both got up and went out of the room. Mum got up and went out too, muttering about making a nice cup of tea. Only Dad and I were left.

'Come on, Alice, cheer up.' Dad had calmed down, and now he came over and put his arm round me. 'It was that Murray woman's fault. She shouldn't have talked you into doing it.'

I nodded, and looked down, so I didn't have to meet Dad's eyes. Melissa hadn't *exactly* talked me into it. I'd been only too willing to do it.

'But it stops right now, Alice,' Dad was saying solemnly. 'No more of this so-called 'real life' stuff, OK?'

'OK,' I muttered.

'Promise?'

'Promise,' I agreed with a sigh. I just couldn't help wondering what Melissa Murray was going to say tomorrow when I told her . . .

Chapter Eleven

'You've done it again, Alice!' Melissa rushed through the front door with a stack of Saturday newspapers in her arms, and grinned triumphantly at me. 'All the reviewers are saying how hilarious last night's programme was!'

'Really?' I said miserably. At the moment I felt anything but hilarious. Sick to my stomach summed things up a whole lot better. I wasn't looking forward to telling Melissa about the promise I'd made to Dad.

'So . . .' Melissa lowered her voice conspiratorially as Nick and Ken went down the hall and into the kitchen with their equipment. 'What did your family think about the programme?'

I bit my lip.

'They weren't very pleased actually . . .'

'Oh dear.' Melissa looked concerned. 'I thought they might be a bit upset, but don't worry. They'll see the funny side eventually. Now –' she took out her notebook, and looked eagerly at me '– what have you got for me this week?'

'Melissa,' I said hesitantly, 'I don't think this is a good idea. And anyway, I promised Dad I wouldn't . . .'

'Alice.' Melissa stepped forward, and put her arm round my shoulders. 'Listen to me. People who work in TV have to be prepared to do things they might not always like to make a point. Do you know what I mean?'

'No . . .'

'Well, take the issue of your dad smoking, for instance.' Melissa looked solemnly at me. 'I mean, I know *you* want him to give up because you're worried about him.'

'Of course I am.'

'Well, then.' Melissa shrugged. 'If he really *does* give up because of last night's programme, then it was worth him being a bit embarrassed, wasn't it?'

I frowned. As I was slowly beginning to realise, the trouble was that Melissa had a knack of making *everything* seem reasonable. Until you went away and thought about it later . . .

'And anyway,' Melissa was saying, 'as I told you before, the viewers are going to like your family a whole lot more if they see that they've got faults just like everybody else.'

'But they must've known *that*, even before last night's programme,' I said. 'After all, there's been enough rowing and arguing going on over the last few weeks. Nobody thinks we're perfect, anyway.'

There was silence for a few seconds.

'Well,' Melissa said reluctantly. 'If you don't want to co-operate, then we can't carry on filming this kind of stuff, can we? We'd better stop right now.'

I felt a wave of relief wash over me.

'Thanks.'

Melissa smiled and shrugged.

'No problem.'

'By the way, I'm going to the park with Albert after breakfast.' I looked hopefully at her. 'D'you want to come and film me?'

'No, I don't think so.' Melissa was turning away from me, and, with a stab of alarm, I could see that she was obviously losing interest. 'I think we've done you and Albert to death now. We need something new to keep the viewers watching.'

I stared at her, feeling a surge of panic at the thought that my fifteen minutes of stardom might already be over. No, it *couldn't* be. Surely the viewers still wanted to see me on the screen?

'I thought – I thought you said I was the Mackenzie the viewers wanted to see at the moment.' Desperately I raced after Melissa, who'd gone into the kitchen where Nick and Ken were making coffee.

'Oh, Alice, that was *last* week.' Melissa shrugged, and reached for the coffee jar. 'You've got to understand that things move fast in TV. What's interesting one week is out of fashion the next. Where's the milk, guys?'

I caught Nick's eye as I stared helplessly at Melissa. He was staring at me grimly, but when he saw me looking at him, he quickly glanced away. What could I do, I asked myself miserably. If I didn't think of something fast, I wasn't going to be Alice Mackenzie, TV star, any more. I was going to be shy, boring, little Alice Mackenzie again, exactly the same as I'd been before . . .

'Well,' I said breathlessly, flinging caution (and my promise to Dad) to the winds, 'I suppose I *might* be able to come up with something. About my family, I mean . . .'

'Really?' Melissa's attention snapped back to me, and I felt a glow of delighted relief. 'That would be marvellous, Alice. Come on, let's go somewhere we can talk in private.' Expertly she propelled me out of the kitchen, and marched me down the hall to the living room. Meanwhile, I was frantically wondering if I'd done the right thing – after all, I *had* promised Dad – but Melissa didn't give me time to change my mind. Briskly she shut the living-room door behind us, flipped open her notebook, and unscrewed her pen.

'Now, I think it would be good if we can actually get a shot of your dad smoking, so I need you to keep your eyes open for that. As for your mum, obviously we'll keep on with the diet-breaking angle, unless you can come up with something new. OK?'

'OK,' I said faintly. I'd really gone and dropped myself in it now. My family, especially my dad, were going to be furious when they found out what I was doing. But if I didn't do it, Melissa and the viewers wouldn't be interested in me any more . . .

Melissa stopped writing, and looked up at me.

'Now, have you got anything more for me on Cindy and Jools?'

'Well, Cindy's going out tonight. And the interesting thing is –' I lowered my voice '– I heard her telling her friend Debbie on the phone that she's bought this really short skirt that's about the size of a face cloth, and she wants to take it round to Debbie's house, and change into it there, so Mum and Dad don't see her.'

Melissa giggled.

'Well, I'm sure we could trail Cindy to Debbie's

house, and then film her coming out in this incredibly short skirt! She won't notice us, if we get hold of a different van.' She made a note in her book. 'OK, anything else?'

'Well, Jools has got a big crush on this girl who works in the chip shop down the road. It might be worth secretly following him down there – his chat-up lines have to be heard to be believed.'

'Good, that'll do to be getting on with.' Melissa snapped her notebook shut quickly as we heard footsteps on the stairs. 'And, Alice, you've made absolutely the right decision to go ahead, you know —'

Just then the living-room door opened, and Dad came in. He did a double-take when he saw Melissa and I standing with our heads together, and then he looked really angry. I gulped, and couldn't help looking guilty.

'Can I have a word, Melissa?' Dad said grimly.

'Have to wait, I'm afraid, Dan.' Melissa breezed airily past him, and went back up the hall. *She* didn't look guilty at all. 'I need to talk to Ken and Nick.'

I went over to put the TV on. I didn't really want to watch it, but it meant I didn't have to face Dad's accusing stare.

'Alice, you *do* remember what we discussed yesterday, don't you?' he said warningly.

'Yes,' I muttered, grabbing the remote control. I was beginning to feel besieged on all sides. And now that I didn't have Melissa standing next to me, and telling me I was doing the right thing, I was beginning to feel guilty again.

'I'm only asking because it looked like you and that Murray woman were cooking something up again.' Although I couldn't look at Dad, I could tell he was staring hard at me. 'You weren't, were you, Alice?'

'No.' I blurted the word out before I could stop myself. But I didn't ever lie to Dad. Not really. Not about big, important things anyway, and so even I could hear the false note in my voice.

There was silence in the room for a few moments. I concentrated hard on the cartoon on the TV screen, guilt eating away at my insides. I hoped Dad would go away, but he didn't. When I finally plucked up enough courage to glance over at him again, the look on his face made me go cold all over. He didn't even look angry though. He just looked upset.

I opened my mouth to say something – anything – but right at the same moment, Dad turned abruptly, and went over to the door.

'Tell your mum I've gone to the match.'

'The match?' I stared at his back. 'But it doesn't

start till three, and it's only half past nine —'

Dad didn't answer. He went out of the living room, and a few minutes later I heard the front door slam. I sat with my mouth open, unable to believe what had just happened. Dad and I never rowed. Well, hardly ever. And he always asked me if I wanted to go to the football match with him on Saturdays. Sometimes I went, and sometimes I didn't, but he'd always *asked*. Until today. A huge sob rose in my throat, but at that moment, Nick, Ken and Melissa came down the hall, and I had to swallow it down.

'OK, let's get set up,' Melissa was saying to the crew. 'So, Alice, what're you going to do today? Are you going to the supermarket with your mum?'

'No,' I muttered. Mum and I weren't getting on too well after last night's programme.

'Are you going round to Francine's then?' Melissa winked at me. 'Maybe *she's* got a few little secrets we could put into this week's programme?'

'Er – no. I'm not going to Francine's today,' I said slowly. Francine and I still hadn't made up properly over that row we had on Monday. Suddenly I was beginning to feel very, very lonely.

'Well, maybe we could film you reading something from your notebook again?' Melissa suggested brightly. 'I think our viewers would like that.'

'OK,' I agreed, wondering why I was feeling so gloomy. After all, I was Alice Mackenzie, TV star now . . .

I went slowly out of the kitchen to fetch my Top Secret Notebook. In the hall I met Mum, on her way to the kitchen with a load of dirty washing.

'All right, love?' she said quietly, but she didn't look any happier than I felt.

Cindy was lying on her bed, reading a magazine when I pushed the door open. She sat bolt upright, and glared at me.

'You haven't brought that nosy TV crew up with you, have you?' she demanded.

'Of course not,' I retorted, going over to my desk.

'Of course not,' Cindy mimicked in a high, squeaky voice. Her eyes narrowed. 'Maybe I ought to go and tell Melissa Murray how you wet yourself the first day you started school? Then *you* can find out for yourself just how it feels to be made a fool of on the telly.'

I stared at her.

'You – you wouldn't . . .'

'Why not?' Cindy turned her back on me, and

picked up her magazine. 'It's only the same thing you've done to the rest of us, isn't it?'

Biting my lip, I went out of the room. Jools's bedroom door was open, and I could see him inside, lying on his bed with his headphones on. But when I stopped and looked in, he got up off his bed, and slammed the door in my face.

I went downstairs, trying not to burst into tears. Being a TV star just wasn't worth all the hassle I was getting. I was going to have to talk to Melissa . . .

The phone in the living room was ringing, but it stopped as soon as I got to the bottom of the stairs. Then I could hear Mum talking.

'What? No. Oh no . . .'

Something in her voice sent an icy shiver all over me. I ran into the living room on legs that were suddenly trembling. Mum was clutching the phone, looking pale and terrified. Melissa, Nick and Ken were in there too. They looked shocked as well, but I noticed that Nick was filming Mum where she stood, as still as a stone.

I tried to speak, but it took me a few seconds to get my voice working properly.

'What's happened?'

'Oh, Alice, it's your dad.' Mum was staring straight at me, but she seemed to be looking right through me. 'He collapsed in the street, and he's been taken to hospital. He's had a heart attack . . .'

Chapter Twelve

Nobody knew whether it was best to keep quiet, or whether it was best to talk on the way to the hospital. We were all trying to keep very calm, so talking was difficult. But keeping quiet was even more difficult because we knew we were all silently thinking the same, terrible thing.

'Mum, Dad isn't going to – isn't going to die, is he?' Cindy's face looked washed out, her black eyelashes huge against her white skin, as she huddled in one corner of the taxi. She spoke quietly, without drama. 'I mean, he's going to be OK – isn't he?'

'Of course he is.' But there was a false note in Mum's voice that sent fear like I'd never experienced before shuddering through me, and I was glad when Mum reached over, and put her arm round me. 'He's going to be fine.'

I chewed painfully at my bottom lip. I didn't look at anyone. I couldn't. All I could think about was the last time I'd seen Dad that morning. When we'd rowed . . . Was that going to be the last time I ever saw him?

I hated myself like I'd never hated myself before. Nothing that had ever happened to me in my whole life had prepared me for this.

'What if he doesn't make it?' Jools muttered, as he stared out of the car window, not looking at anybody.

'He *will*,' Mum said, more strongly this time. Nobody answered. We all knew she was saying it as much to convince herself as to reassure us.

A huge sob welled up painfully in my throat. I turned away to swallow it down, and glanced out of the back window of the taxi. Then I sat up, my eyes wide. A white van, with the familiar blue and red 'Harlequin TV' logo on the side, was chasing along behind us. Ken was in the driver's seat, with Melissa and Nick sitting next to him. They were following us to the hospital. A deep, sour bitterness that surprised even me sprang up inside me. Our dad might be dying – and they were coming to *film* it?

I opened my mouth to say something to the others, but just then the taxi swept up to the hospital steps. We all bundled out quickly, and Mum and Cindy hurried through the swing doors, ahead of Jools and me. I grabbed his arm.

'Look, Melissa's right behind us,' I whispered to him shakily.

Jools glanced over his shoulder, and swore.

'Come on, they won't get past the hospital security anyway,' he hissed, his face dark with fury. 'Don't say anything to Mum.'

I nodded as we followed the others inside to the reception desk.

'My husband Daniel Mackenzie was brought in about an hour ago,' Mum was saying to the receptionist in a trembling voice. 'He – he had a heart attack.'

'Oh, dear, I am sorry.' The nurse at the desk gave us a sympathetic look, and flipped efficiently though her notes. 'Ah, yes, Doctor Sharma is waiting to have a word with you.'

Mum, Cindy and Jools set off at a run down the slippery corridor. At first I followed them, but then I skidded to a halt, and looked round. Melissa, Nick and Ken were just hurrying through the swing doors, complete with filming equipment.

'Hey! Where d' you think you're going?' A burly security guard came over immediately to block their path, eyeing them suspiciously.

'Melissa Murray, Harlequin TV,' Melissa said confidently, trying to push her way past him.

'We're filming the Mackenzie family right at this very moment, so if you don't mind —'

'No filming in the hospital without permission,' the security guard said firmly.

'Oh, we've got permission,' Melissa said airily, lying through her teeth.

The security guard folded his arms.

'*Written* permission,' he said, raising a smug eyebrow.

A hand fell on my shoulder.

'Come on, squirt,' said Jools urgently.

I pointed at Melissa and the security guard, who were now in the middle of a full-scale row.

'See that?' I said in a voice that shook. 'They just won't leave us alone!'

'They probably don't want to miss out on a death-bed scene,' Jools said brutally, glaring at Melissa. 'That's bound to make "great television".'

'Don't,' I muttered, my stomach twisting into a great, painful knot inside me.

'Sorry.' Jools took my hand, and pulled me away. 'Come on, never mind them. Dad's all that matters.'

We hurried away, leaving Melissa arguing with the security guard behind us, and found Mum and Cindy waiting in another corridor, outside an office.

'What's happening?' Jools asked immediately.

'A nurse told us to wait here to see the doctor,' Mum said shakily.

'She said that Dad's OK, at the moment,' Cindy added, a bit more cheerfully.

We stood there in silence in the white-painted corridor, waiting for the doctor. I glanced at Mum. She looked frozen and pale and pinched, and, suddenly, a whole lot older. Strangely, Jools and Cindy, who stood protectively on either side of her, looked much younger than usual. Cindy had mascara streaked down both cheeks, and, for once, Jools had taken his shades off, and put them in his pocket.

I leaned my aching head against the cool, white corridor wall, and thought about what would happen if my dad died. Everything would be different. My whole life would change. And I'd stupidly thought that being on TV was so important. That I could change the world, just by being a TV star. It was nothing compared to how my own world would change if Dad died . . .

I squeezed my eyes tightly shut as memories cut painfully through my thoughts like a knife. Dad buying me my first bike. Dad winning the fathers' race at Sports Day. The time when, aged six, I had been out shopping with Dad and had lost my favourite doll. Dad had spent hours retracing our steps until we found it. Our holiday in Wales when Dad taught me to swim. Emotions that were too strong and hurt too much for me even to be able to cry flooded through me. Suddenly my whole life seemed brought into sharper focus, just as if I was looking at it through the lens of a TV camera.

I opened my eyes – and that was when I saw them. Melissa, Nick and Ken standing a little way down the corridor, with the camera pointed in our direction. I was startled. For a moment I thought I was seeing things. Then I realised what must have happened. Melissa, with her confident line in chat, had obviously managed to talk her way in past hospital security.

I glanced at Mum, Jools and Cindy. They hadn't noticed the camera yet, but they soon would. A slow, burning anger rose up inside me. What was happening now was something private. Something personal. Something which shouldn't be filmed. Melissa might go on and on about the fact that we'd signed a contract, but there were some things that were outside all that. This was one of them.

With a sudden flash of insight, I realised that, although Melissa probably liked us all and was quite fond of us by now, that wouldn't stop her from filming. If Dad really was dying, it still wouldn't stop her. Nothing would. Because, like she'd always said, she wanted to make 'great television', and if that meant using me to find out my family's secrets, she would. If it meant muscling in on a family who didn't know if their father was going to live or die, she'd do it. And she'd justify it by saying that it would be great TV.

But this wasn't TV. It wasn't drama and it wasn't soap opera. This was real life. *My* real life. Mum's and Cindy's and Jools's real life. And Dad's . . .

I stood upright, and then walked purposefully off down the corridor towards Melissa.

'Alice! Where are you going —' I heard Mum's voice behind me tail off as she noticed the film crew.

I went straight up to Melissa, and stopped in front of her. She looked at me sympathetically, but I knew her well enough now to recognise a spark of interest in her eyes, as she wondered what I was going to say.

'Go away,' I said, surprising myself by how steady my voice sounded. 'You shouldn't be here.'

There was silence for a second or two. Nobody moved.

'Go away,' I said again. '*Please.*'

'Alice, we know how you feel, believe me.' Melissa smiled gently at me. 'We won't get in the way, don't worry.'

'Go away,' I repeated, my voice starting to wobble a bit now. Why couldn't they see that we didn't want them there?

Then something strange happened. Nick lowered his camera, and looked me straight in the eye for a second or two. Then he turned abruptly, and walked off down the corridor without a word.

Melissa's mouth fell open, and so did mine.

'Nick!' she called after him. ' Nick! Where are you going?'

'Could you keep your voice down, please?' snapped an acid-faced nurse who was just walking past. 'This *is* a hospital, you know.'

'Er – sorry.' Melissa looked more flustered than I'd ever seen her look before. 'Nick! Wait!'

She raced off down the corridor after him, and I breathed a trembly sigh of relief.

'Hope your dad's OK, Alice,' Ken said quietly, before he hurried after her.

I watched them right to the end of the corridor until they all turned the corner, just to make sure they were really gone. Then I heard a voice behind me, a cool, calm, reassuring voice.

‘Mrs Mackenzie? I’m Doctor Sharma. About your husband . . .’

Chapter Thirteen

'Would you like another cup of tea, Dad?'

'No, I'm fine, thanks, Ally.'

'What about a piece of toast then?'

'I've had one already, love.'

'Well, shall I go out and get you a newspaper?'

'I'm fine, Ally. Honestly.' Dad smiled at me, and patted the garden chair next to him. 'Come and sit down, and talk to me instead.'

I sat down next to him, with Albert in my arms. Although it was still quite early in the morning, the sun was already warm on my face, and the sky was a deep, unbroken blue. We were sitting on the patio in our tiny back garden, and looking out over all the yellow and white daffodils that Mum had planted last year.

It was three weeks since Dad had had the heart attack, and now he was home for good. The doctor had said he was going to be OK, but he definitely had to give up smoking now, and no arguments.

'Listen to that racket going on inside,' Dad

grumbled, sticking his fingers in his ears. 'I can hardly believe it's all over, you know.'

The reason why we were sitting out in the back garden was to escape from the hordes of engineers who'd arrived from Harlequin TV to pull up the electric cables, and pack away all the equipment. The six weeks were finally over, and filming in the Mackenzie household had finished at last. Right now, I didn't know whether to feel glad or sorry.

There'd been three more programmes shown since Dad had been ill. Programmes four, five and six had been mostly about Dad's heart attack, and how the family had coped. They'd even kept the scene in at the hospital when I'd asked Melissa to leave, which had surprised me a bit.

Even though we'd all been so worried about Dad, the last few programmes had, in a way, been the best of all. It had been good for people to see that there was another side to the Mackenzie family. Dad had really been shaken by the heart attack, and so while he'd been in the hospital, we'd all rallied round to try and cheer him up. We'd visited him every day, and Cindy, Jools and I had taken over all the housework and the cooking, so that Mum could spend all the time she wanted to with Dad. Cindy and Jools had even given up their social lives to stay in and help out. It had been really hard for Cindy in particular, because she had her GCSEs coming up, and she was trying to revise. But everybody had done their best, and that was typical of the Mackenzies. OK, maybe on the surface we were an annoying lot, but when there was a crisis, we really stuck together as a family.

'By the way, Ally,' Dad said with a teasing grin, 'I hear you're still a bit of a star with the viewing millions . . .'

I blushed. There'd been a lot of fuss in the newspapers about me asking the TV crew to leave the hospital. Letters and phone calls had poured into the Harlequin offices about how right I'd been, and what a heroine I was (again). Funnily enough, though, I didn't care. I'd been too worried about Dad to bother about being a TV superstar.

'Oh, that . . .' Feeling embarrassed, I glanced sideways at him. I knew there were some things I had to say, but there just hadn't been any time to say them over the last few weeks. I'd apologised properly to Mum, Cindy and Jools, but I really needed to sort things out with Dad, before I felt right. Now seemed like a good time. 'Dad?'

'Yes, Ally?'

'Sorry.' I paused, and took a deep breath. I could see from his face that Dad knew what I meant, but I wanted to say it anyway. 'Sorry for being such a brat before.'

Dad slid his arm round me.

'I know. But it wasn't all your fault. I think you had quite a bit of encouragement from you-know-who.'

I nodded. I'd realised at the hospital that Melissa Murray had been using me all the time to get what she wanted for her programme. But a lot of it was still my fault. I could have stopped things any time I wanted, if I hadn't got so obsessed with the idea of being a star. So I'd almost forgiven Melissa. Almost, but not quite.

'Anyway,' Dad went on comfortingly, 'we were *all* brats at one time or another while we were doing that programme. Look at me, being all dramatic, and throwing my cigarettes in the dustbin, when secretly I had no intention of giving up!' He sighed. 'I suppose being on TV really went to our heads.'

I nodded sheepishly.

'I suppose it did.'

'But it was worth it in the end, wasn't it?' Dad went on. 'We've all learned something about ourselves over the last six weeks, including you.' He looked at me solemnly. 'You've learned that you're not so quiet and shy after all. In fact, you've got more nerve than Cindy's ever had!'

I sat in silence, stroking Albert's head and thinking. Dad was right. I'd learnt a lot about myself over the last few weeks. Some of it I didn't like very much . . . But I'd done some good things too. I'd found the courage to rescue Albert, and I'd done that because I'd wanted to, not because I thought it would make me into a TV star. When I'd asked the TV crew to leave the hospital, I hadn't been thinking of myself then either. I'd been too worried about Dad. So one thing was for sure. I was never going to think of myself as the most shy, quiet, boring member of the Mackenzie family again.

'And you were definitely right about one thing,' Dad said with a grin. 'I should've given up smoking ages ago!'

The back door opened just then, and Mum, Cindy and Jools trooped out into the garden one by one, followed by Francine.

'The TV crew are nearly ready to leave,' Mum said, coming over to us. 'Melissa said she'd pop out to say goodbye before she goes.'

'That should set my recovery back by several months,' Dad murmured, winking at me.

'Hi, France.' I moved up so that Francine could squash onto the chair with me and Albert. She'd come round straightaway when she'd heard about Dad's heart attack, and we'd made up after our argument. I was glad. Being a TV star didn't mean much, if you lost your best mate.

'Hi. Hello, Mr Mackenzie.' Francine grinned at us. 'I bet you're all *really* sorry that the TV people are going today, aren't you?'

'Not me.' Jools shook his head. He'd been OK ever since he'd managed to convince his mates that Boris the teddy bear had been planted under his bed by Cindy in an attempt to shame him. 'I'll be glad to see the back of them.'

'Yeah, thank God it's all over, that's what I say.' Cindy perched on the garden table, and examined her fingernails with a bored look. 'I think being on TV is definitely over-rated.'

'Me too,' Dad said fervently.

'I can't say I'm sorry either,' Mum said with a sigh. 'I really can't believe everything that's happened over the last six weeks.'

'Me neither,' I muttered, biting my lip. 'I still feel really awful about it.'

'Oh, we were all just as bad,' Cindy said, rolling her eyes. 'When I think what we were like . . .'

'Yeah, me and my purple hair,' Jools chimed in. 'I've only just managed to wash the last bit of colour out.'

‘I know,’ said Mum grimly. ‘Every towel we own is now covered in purple streaks !’

We all started giggling.

‘Oh, well,’ said Cindy. ‘We’ve survived it, haven’t we?’

‘Just,’ said Dad quietly, and everyone was silent for a minute or two. That reminded me of something I had to do, and I stood up, plonking Albert onto Francine’s lap.

‘Back in a minute,’ I said mysteriously. ‘I’ve got to see a man about a camera . . .’

I went inside, and into the kitchen. Nick was on his own in there, winding up cables. I hadn’t had a chance to get him on his own before without Melissa being around, and I wanted to say thanks for what he’d done at the hospital. I stopped in the kitchen doorway, waited for him to look up and see me, and then smiled uncertainly.

‘All right?’ he said gruffly, and carried on winding.

‘Um – I just wanted to say thank you,’ I stammered, hopping from one foot to the other in embarrassment. ‘For not filming at the hospital, I mean . . .’

‘’S’all right.’ Nick looked up briefly, and nodded at me.

'You – er – you won't lose your job or anything, will you?' I asked anxiously.

Nick made a funny noise, like a bark. At first I thought he was coughing, then I realised he was laughing.

'Nope. I'm the only person who'd put up with Melissa Murray for five minutes.'

'So why did you do it?' I asked curiously.

Nick shrugged. Just for a moment it looked as if he was going to answer me, but then he turned and walked past me out of the kitchen.

'Got to go,' he said abruptly. 'See you.'

I stared down the hall after him. Now I'd never know why he'd done it. Maybe he'd been in the same situation himself once, standing in a hospital corridor, waiting to find out if his dad was going to live or die. Who knows? Anyway, I was grateful.

I went back out into the garden, just as Melissa Murray came up the path at the side of the house.

'I've checked all our equipment back into the vans,' she announced with a dazzling smile, 'and we're just about ready to leave.'

I stared hard at her. She didn't seem to be at all guilty about anything that had happened – the way she'd manipulated me into showing up my family on TV, the way she'd followed us to the hospital after Dad's heart attack. And maybe she didn't *feel* guilty. Maybe she thought that her job of making TV programmes was so important that she could do anything she liked. Well, I didn't. And, personally, I wouldn't be sorry if I didn't see Melissa Murray again for a very long time.

Melissa was standing in the middle of the patio, making a speech as usual.

'– and it's been marvellous working with you all. The series has been very well received, and *so* popular with the viewers.'

'I'm glad it's all turned out well,' said Mum. 'But I can't say I'll be sorry to have the house to ourselves again.'

'I can't wait!' Cindy announced languidly. 'I'm fed up with being in the public eye all the time.'

'Yeah, it'll be excellent being able to slob out in front of the telly, without wondering if you're going to get filmed,' Jools agreed.

I nodded.

'I'm glad it's all over too,' I said. 'Being a child superstar was starting to get on my nerves.'

Melissa looked uncertainly at us, as if she wasn't sure whether we were joking or not.

'Well, I hope the experience hasn't been *too* off-putting for you, because – well, this is extremely hush-hush and I shouldn't really be saying a word yet . . . But Cameron is keen on us making another series of *Happy Families* next year. You know, do a kind of update – see how you're getting on, and what's changed over the last twelve months.'

There was silence for a moment, and then –

'Really?' gasped Mum, beaming all over her face. 'That would be marvellous!'

'Brilliant!' Cindy squealed. 'I can't wait!'

'Maybe you could come back every year, and film us till we're grown-up,' Jools suggested breathlessly.

'What about you, Alice?' Melissa looked at me enquiringly. 'Do *you* like the idea?'

I couldn't help smiling, especially when I glanced over at Dad. I could see by his face that he was excited by the idea too. And so was I.

'Well,' I said, 'I think I could probably cope.'